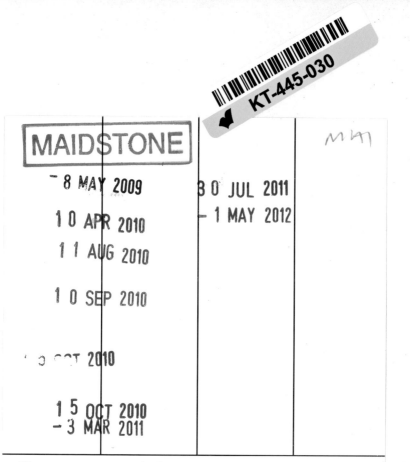

KT-445-030

M M

Please return on or before the latest date above.
You can renew online at *www.kent.gov.uk/libs*
or by telephone 08458 247 200

CUSTOMER SERVICE EXCELLENCE

Libraries & Archives

00884\DTP\RN\07.07   LIB 7

What every parent should know...
before their child
goes to
secondary school

Jane Bidder

Editor: Roni Jay

new tricks for old dogs

Published by White Ladder Press Ltd

Great Ambrook, Near Ipplepen, Devon TQ12 5UL

01803 813343

www.whiteladderpress.com

First published in Great Britain in 2007

10 9 8 7 6 5 4 3 2

© Jane Bidder 2007

The right of Jane Bidder to be identified as author of this work has been asserted by her in accordance with the Copyright, Designs and Patents Act 1988.

ISBN 978 1 905410 20 0

British Library Cataloguing in Publication Data

A CIP record for this book can be obtained from the British Library.

Designed and typeset by Julie Martin Ltd
Cover design by Julie Martin Ltd
Cover photograph Jonathon Bosley
Printed and bound by TJ International Ltd, Padstow, Cornwall
Cover printed by St Austell Printing Company
Printed on totally chlorine-free paper
The paper used for the text pages of this book is FSC certified.
FSC (The Forest Stewardship Council) is an international
network to promote responsible management of the world's forests.

FSC
Mixed Sources
Product group from well-managed
forests and other controlled sources

Cert no. SGS-COC-2482
www.fsc.org
© 1996 Forest Stewardship Council

White Ladder books are distributed in the UK by Virgin Books

White Ladder Press
Great Ambrook, Near Ipplepen, Devon TQ12 5UL
01803 813343
www.whiteladderpress.com

Contents

Why you need this book

We're not going to start by spouting all that old rubbish about school days being the happiest days of your life. If you're lucky, they may well have been. But if they weren't, the chances are that you're still being affected by it even if you're middle-aged and balding (we're not speaking for ourselves, of course).

But whether you loved school or not, we wouldn't mind betting that it was one of the biggest factors in your life. And that's why we parents spend most of our lives wondering – all right, obsessing – over which school is right for our child.

The choices are huge, aren't they? And because today's parents are so keen to do the best for their children, it's not always easy to know which educational route is best. Private or state? Close or local? A school which is academic so will push your child but might also make them feel inadequate if everyone was better than them? A school which is not so academic and will make your child feel good about themselves but not stretch them? Single sex or mixed? The list is endless.

One point which we often forget is that every child is different. Your neighbour might swear blind that School X round the corner did her kids proud, but it might not be right for your own little prodigy (or should that be rebel?).

My three children are both similar and different from each other. They've all had experience of state and private at different times in their lives. And we've also gone through the trauma of the 11 and 12 plus because at the time, we lived in a county with grammar schools.

It wouldn't be fair to say which child had what kind of experience or they wouldn't speak to me again. But I did learn that not all children can cope with being moved from a small secure environment to a big state school where the loos didn't lock properly and kids frequently got beaten up by the neighbouring rival schoolkids.

I also learned that you can get your child into a good grammar school outside your catchment area in the sixth form, where there might be more flexibility about where you live.

It also helps if you and your partner agree on what kind of school you want your child to go to. We don't want to sound moralistic here but do try to listen to each other's feelings. Your other half might be adamant about your son going to a mixed school because they didn't learn to talk to the opposite sex before the age of 18. But you're worried your son might be distracted by subjects that aren't on the National Curriculum.

Choosing the right school is a bit like getting pregnant. You think that's the be all and end all, but when you get your child into the school of your choice, it's actually just the beginning. Now you've got all those other problems in front of you. Just wait until your offspring gets homework phobia; doesn't make nice friends; is convinced the teachers hate them; and can't get to grip with maths.

The good news is that we can help you with all this and more. We're not promising to achieve 100 per cent. But this is a book you'll dip in and out of throughout your child's school life. Much of our advice comes from parents like ourselves as well as teachers and other 'experts'. And if you want to know what happened to my three, the older two went on to great universities and the youngest has just started working harder because he's suddenly remembered he's got GCSEs this summer…

CHAPTER 1

Choosing the right school for your child

Where do we start? There are so many things to consider when it comes to choosing the right school for our kids, that it's no wonder parents get confused. It's also much more complicated nowadays than when we were young. There are so many options available, thanks to recent government schemes, that it's hard to know which is best.

So we're going to do what we tell our kids. In other words, start at the beginning. It's not quite as simple as ABC but hang on in there and you'll hopefully get the picture.

Do your homework

We said we'd start with the simple stuff, didn't we? Phone or write to your local education authority (LEA) and ask for a list of all the schools in the area. The booklet will also contain information about the schools, their admission arrangements, their popularity, how many pupils they admit and so on.

Each school will also publish its own prospectus. You'll need to ring up each school to get one.

Location, location, location

More simple stuff. It matters where the school is. If your child's new secondary school involves a long journey, they will be tired at the end of the day. This means they'll need to rest before homework and then they might be too tired to do it at all. The following morning, they'll have to get up earlier to get there on time so they'll be half asleep when they get there. The result – surprise, surprise – is that they won't be able to concentrate as well as they might if they'd had more sleep. Trust me. I've been through this one. I once had a 40 minute school run to each of two different schools. Times that by four and you can see why we eventually moved house.

The other point about the school's location is that if it's near your home, your child is more likely to know other kids who are starting at the same time. They'll also know older children who might just, if you're lucky, keep an eye on them. And even if your child doesn't like these kids particularly or considers them 'sad',

"Look, it's only three train journeys and two buses. And a bit of a hike at the other end. But you'll be back home before midnight. And it's a brilliant school."

they might think differently when they see a familiar face on that first day.

Finally, from a parent's point of view, it makes life so much easier if you're near school because you don't have to do long mercy rush school runs when your child rings from school to say they've forgotten their maths homework/sports kit and can you possibly bring it in. I used to do this – yes, I know I'm a sucker – but now we live five minutes away from my son's secondary school, he can leg it home himself to retrieve missing items.

If you're lucky, there might be a bus to school. But it's up to your local education authority to decide if your child is entitled to free transport. School transport is free to all children between five and 16 who go to their nearest suitable school and who live further away than the law says they should walk. This is two miles for children who are aged eight or under and three miles for children aged eight and over.

TOP TIP

If you've read the above para instead of skipping it, you'll see that free transport stops at 16. Like many parents, this one took me by surprise when I suddenly found myself forking out for the bus fare. It wasn't cheap...

THE EXPERTS SAY...

"I'd recommend choosing a school near your home," says Sue Foreman, mother and national executive member of the National Association of Schoolmasters Union of Women Teachers (NASUWT). "It means children get less tired and it's also where their peers are more likely to go. It's a big step from primary to secondary schools and the more links they have, the better."

Reputation

Schools are like people. You often hear of their reputation before you meet them. And this isn't always a good thing. One parent's meat is often another parent's poison. So if a well meaning mum or dad tells you that School A is rubbish, don't accept that verdict until you've judged it for yourself. Children are different. School A might not suit their child. But it could be just the ticket for yours.

Most parents who've done their homework start with the Ofsted report. You can get a copy of this through your local education authority (address in the phone book), the library or online (just Google 'Ofsted' and go from there.) This might give you some flavour but don't treat it as gospel. Like other parents' verdicts, it can't give you the full picture.

The same goes for Achievement and Attainment Tables, formerly known as the Performance Table and commonly known as League tables. Now these seemed a good idea at the time but, in reality, they're the bane of many a teacher's life – and they don't always help parents. School A might appear high up on the listings of league tables, but this doesn't necessarily mean it has fantastic results. Some schools will discourage pupils from staying on if their grades are going to drag the rest of the results down. So the position in the league table might not actually reflect the true overall performance.

Secondary School Tables come in two sets. One shows the results of Key Stage 3 tests, plus a measure of value added between Key Stages 2 and 3 for all maintained secondary schools in England. The other set covers results in GCSEs and equivalent, plus other vocational qualifications, and shows the value added between Key Stages 2 and 3, and on to GCSEs and equivalent for all schools.

Also, log onto the school's website. You can find this out by Googling its name. Websites can tell you quite a lot. A well laid out website suggests the school knows how to present itself. Does it have a welcoming attitude? What facts and figures does it tell you? What does it leave out? Use this information to ask questions when you look around.

Finally, there's nothing like judging a book by its cover. Personally, I like to take a good look at the kids who go to the school, in order to judge its reputation. I'm not talking about their appearance – any decent self-respecting teenager looks as though the cat has dragged them in. No, I'm talking articulation here. Are the kids who go to School A able to talk without too many grunts? Can they tell you what they like and dislike about the teachers? Would they recommend it? If not, why? And can you understand them or do they have a fag in their mouth at the same time?

Pay a visit

We're great believers in following your gut feelings in life. And schools are no exceptions. Go and visit the schools on your short list and take your victim with you. If possible, we'd recommend leaving younger children behind. I still cringe with embarrassment when I remember my youngest having a tantrum in the headmaster's office because he wasn't getting any attention, while his brother was being interviewed..

Most secondary schools have open days or evenings. Go to those too. But also ring up and ask if you can look around individually. You'll learn more this way than on a formal day when the pupils will have been told to wash their hair/shave/stop grunting. If you're truly clever, you could turn up on the wrong day and really catch them out. I did this once by mistake but the headmistress was good enough to still show me round. As she said, I could see it as it really was without any pretence.

Visitor's checklist

- Make a list of the questions you want to ask during your visit. Here are some examples:

- What's your policy on bullying?

- What happens if my child falls behind with work? Do you automatically inform me?

- Are there 'maths clinics' etc at lunchtime for those who need extra help?

- How do you help new children adjust to the different demands of secondary school? For example, do you give them advice on organising themselves/ doing homework on time/revision?

- What options are available at Year 9? This might sound a long way off but if your child loves history and geography but the school curriculum will only allow them to choose one option for GCSE, you might like to know before they start.

- How many children are there in the class?

- How many hours of sport a week is available?

- Are there breakfast clubs/after school clubs?

- If your child has a special interest, such as music, what facilities are there?

- How does their pastoral care system operate? What do they do if children find it hard to settle?

- If your child has special needs, what extra provisions are there? What special provisions are there if your child is dyslexic?

- What should you do, as a parent, if you're not happy with a particular teacher? Is there a standard complaints procedure? (You won't make yourself popular with this one but it will come in handy. See also Chapter Eighteen on how to handle difficult teachers.)

Also make your own general observations.

- Do the children look happy?

- Do the staff look happy? This is more important than the state of the paintwork on the walls. Or maybe they're climbing up them…

- Was the school welcoming?

- Do you think it would suit your child?

- What are the school's values? If it's very churchy, for example, this might not be right for you. Or it could be just what you're looking for.

Same sex or different?

Do you have set ideas on single or mixed sex schools? If so, you might like to think again. Often, we make these decisions based on our own experience. Just because we went to an all girls or all boys school and found ourselves unable to talk properly to the opposite sex for the next 20 years, doesn't mean we should only consider mixed sex schools for our own kids.

Talk to your children and see what they want. Go and look at different sex schools – that doesn't sound right but you know what we mean. Keep an open mind.

A recent survey carried out on behalf of the Headmasters' and Headmistresses' Conference shows that single sex schooling makes no difference to a child's academic performance. However, there's a growing belief in the United States that boys' and girls' brains develop differently so that single sex schools are of benefit to both.

"I teach in a school where it is mixed until the sixth form. I've often noticed that boys who were behind girls in the early years picked up when they were in a class with brighter girls. I think this is because you do better when you are surrounded by clever children." **Teacher who declined to be named**

TOP TIP

74 per cent of parents of secondary school children do not know if their sons or daughters have lost their virginity. Forty four per cent admit they never talk about sex in any detail with their child. *From a survey commissioned for Teacher's TV*

Is it a good match?

Taking into account all these points, you need to sit down with a pen, paper and – optionally – a stiff drink. The aim is to see if the schools on your short list are a good match for your child. Write down a pros and cons list. For example, it's got a strong English department but it involves a long journey. Then get your child to do the same. They might raise something you hadn't thought of. In our painful experience, kids excel at that. Don't make up your mind then and there. Go to bed and sleep on it for a few nights.

Take it from us

"When we moved to a new area, I wasn't keen on our local comprehensive because one of my neighbours discredited it. But then I met someone else who said their son was very happy there. I spoke to him and he told me why he liked it. Then I went to look round and was most impressed. If I hadn't listened to the second person, I would have dismissed it."
Mother of three from London

"Think about whether the school is one that your child would be happy in. For example, does it have an atmosphere and culture that your child will be comfortable in? Can they get there independently? Does it encourage parents to be involved? Is there a sound pastoral system in place (anti-bullying etc)? Does it value the things that your child does? If they are musical, does the school celebrate music? I think these things turn out to be of more importance in the long run than whether their friends are going there as well."
Sandra, Brighton

"Speak to like-minded parents whose children are already at the school. Ask them what they like and dislike. No school is perfect. And what suits one child, might not suit another."
Judy, Winchester

"Schools' reputations can change. School B might have been a lost cause five years ago but a new head might have turned it around since then. So don't cross it off your list." *Sandy, Birmingham*

"My son had dyspraxia and dyslexia so I needed a school with special needs provision. I also wanted one with the right sort of atmosphere where he wouldn't be teased and bullied, as he was previously." *Name withheld*

"Talk to friends who applied to schools the year before. Their advice will be fresh and up to date." *Sue, Staines*

"My daughter's school is Catholic and I like its old-fashioned values. It's very good at communicating with parents and children." *Maria, Basingstoke*

"Decide what's important to you, for your child's education, and do the research to find the best match." *Jan, Hertfordshire*

"I am a teacher and my husband is a primary school inspector so we knew what we were looking for when choosing a secondary school for our children. Go round the school yourself, ideally without an official tour although obviously with a member of staff. Look at the environment in which the children work. Have a look at their exercise books as you go through the classrooms. Try to talk to the children about what they're doing. Stand at the school gate and watch the way in which the children leave. Talk to other parents in the area. Go to open days. Watch to see if most pupils get at least five A-C results at GCSE over as many years as you can. Look at the policy re the teaching of science and the languages." *Name withheld*

"Take your child with you when you visit a school. Observe the attitude of teaching staff toward your child. Personally, I have to like the head teacher. And don't be taken in by nice buildings." *Anne, York*

"Don't be too swayed by league tables – the school's results vary with the calibre of students that year." *Kim, Staines*

"In my view, it's better to send your child to a decent state school than scrape together the fees for a mediocre private school. The lower end of the scale simply cannot afford the facilities of state-funded establishments. It's a generalisation

but they tend also to attract duff teachers, presumably because they don't pay so well. I wouldn't personally send my kids to a school that didn't have a uniform, apart from the sixth form. It's an important part of the pride the school feels in itself. It also solves the problem of one-upmanship etc."
Mel, London

"Visit a school twice. Once with your child and once without."
Susan, Cheshire

"Ask what the school does after GCSEs and A levels. This might seem a long time off but I personally am more impressed with schools who arrange things for pupils to do after exams." *Helen, Minehead*

"Ask local shopkeepers what they think of certain schools."
Name withheld

Interesting findings to bear in mind when making your choice

- Worried about class size? The bigger the better according to an all-boys school in south east London. Staff knocked down a wall between two classrooms to teach two classes at the same time. Exam grades were subsequently higher. Coincidence or what?

- The average class size in state secondary schools is 24.9 and around 10-15 in private schools.

- A new survey by York University (new at the time of going to press) suggests that pupils in the sixth form of private schools do just as well as pupils in the sixth form of state schools.

CHAPTER 2

A school by every other name...

In our day, 'school' was called 'school'. Nowadays, we have foundation schools, voluntary controlled schools, voluntary aided schools and even academies. And that's to name but a few.

You may not have all of these choices in your area. In fact, you probably won't. But you might well come across them at some stage. So here's a brief rundown. According to the experts we interviewed, there aren't always any obvious pros and cons to each. But we've flagged up any clear advantages and disadvantages.

Community schools

These are bog standard state schools as we know them. They are run by the local authority which employs the staff and owns the school building and land. It's also responsible for admission procedures and standards. And – very important – they're free.

Foundation schools

These schools are run by a governing body which could, for example, be made up of parents, representatives from the community and representatives of the local authority. This governing body sets its own admission procedures and standards. The school building itself and land is owned either by this body or by a charitable foundation.

Voluntary aided schools

These are usually faith schools, run by a governing body. It's up to that body to decide on entrance requirements. Until recently, this has normally been limited to pupils whose parents belong to that faith. But at the time of going to press, the government has decided that such schools have to take a percentage of children outside that faith. Voluntary aided schools are assisted by the diocese but the staff are employed by the local authority. The land and buildings are normally owned by a charitable foundation but the governing body will contribute towards the cost of maintaining the school buildings.

Voluntary controlled schools

Here, the local authority employs the school staff and decides on admission procedures. The land and buildings are normally owned by a charitable foundation.

Specialist schools

These are state schools which specialise in certain subjects such as sport, languages or technology. In fact, there are 10 specialisms available: arts, business & enterprise, engineering, humanities, languages, mathematics & computing, music, science, sports and technology. Schools can also combine two specialisms. They also have to meet the National Curriculum requirements. So if you've got a child who's particularly talented in a certain area and you can match the school with this talent, this might be for you. At the time of going to press, there are over 2,500 specialist schools. That's over 75 per cent of all secondary schools.

THE EXPERTS SAY...

"The big advantage of some of these new look schools is that they're often in brand new buildings," says Margaret Morrissey, spokesperson for the Parents Teachers Association (PTA). "For some reason, they seem to get better results. Maybe it's because staff go in with a more positive attitude and have the resources available. Be careful, however, if you send your child to a specialist school and he or she doesn't particularly enjoy the specialist area. Although the school will also do other subjects too, there'll be an emphasis on that specialisation and your child could feel out of it."

Maintained boarding schools

Boarding schools aren't just for the private sector. A number of state maintained schools also have boarding facilities. Parents are charged only for boarding. The tuition is free. For more information, see the Department for Education and Skills' leaflet 'Parents' Guide to Maintained Boarding Schools'. You can download it from the DFES website or contact the DFES on 01325 391272.

Special schools

These are run by the local education authority for children with special educational needs, otherwise known as SEN. However, nowadays many SEN children go to mainstream schools.

Trust schools

Trust schools are funded by the government but get extra support from a charitable trust such as an educational charity, community group or local business.

Extended schools

These are schools which have facilities like breakfast clubs and after-school clubs, as well as programmes for the community, usually outside school hours. So they're good news for working parents. They might also have sport and music clubs, and even health care such as speech therapy. According to the DFES web-site, there is evidence that extended services can help to:

- Improve pupil attendance, self-confidence and motivation and pupil attainment.

- Reduce exclusion rates.

- Better enable teachers to focus on teaching and learning.

- Enhance children's and families access to services.

Academies

These are independent schools sponsored by the public. For example, they could be run by a large company or charitable trust. Education is free. In theory, they sound fantastic. But some people have their reservations. "They seem to be able to do what they like," says Margaret Morrissey, spokesperson for the Parents Teachers Association. "What happens if the sponsoring body decides it doesn't want to be in education any more? That could mean the school might close."

City technology colleges

Also known as CTCs. These are non-fee paying schools for pupils of all abilities in urban areas. They are designed to prepare pupils for the working world and provide vocational qualifications for pupils over 16 as well as A levels or equivalents.

Independent schools

Also known as private schools or public schools. There are about 2,300 in England and details can be obtained from the Independent Schools Council, St Vincent House, 30 Orange Street, London WC2H 7HH. Tel 020 7766 7070. Or email office@isc.co.uk.

Independent schools are, surprise, surprise, independently run and financed by school fees and investments. Some have charitable status. Independent schools have to be registered with the Department for Education and Skills and reach certain standards. They can provide a curriculum that's outside the National Curriculum and set their own fees and holiday dates. There are also several scholarships available. For more information, see The Directory of Grant Making Trusts available from the Charities Aid Foundation, Kings Hill, West Malling, Kent ME19 4TA.

Selective schools

There are three kinds of selective schools in the state system. In other words, schools which can choose which kind of pupils to take, depending on their abilities.

Partially selective schools

These are schools which already had an existing partially selective admission arrangement during the 1997/8 school year. They are allowed to continue with this as long as there is no change in the method of selection or the proportion of pupils selected. Under the scheme, they are allowed to select a certain number of pupils on the basis of their ability or aptitude.

Grammar schools

There is still a small number of local education authorities (LEAs) which have grammar schools. There may be one test at the age of 11 or 12 to assess your child's ability or schools might run their own tests. Grammar schools appear to perform very favourably in league tables.

TOP TIP

If your child fails to get in first time round, they can sit the entrance exam again in later years. Talk to the school and local education authority.

Banding

Some comprehensive schools use banding to make sure they have a selection of pupils of all abilities. Children who want to go there are tested to see where their strengths and weaknesses lie, and are then put into the ability band which matches their results. However, if a particular band is oversubscribed, the school is not allowed to choose the children with the best result. Instead, the normal admission criteria for that school has to be followed. The advantage of this is that children are put into the right 'set' for their subjects.

Northern Ireland

Here, education is administered centrally by the Department of Education and, locally, in controlled schools by Education and Library Boards. As well as controlled schools, there are voluntary maintained schools which are mainly under Roman Catholic management and voluntary grammar schools which take Protestant and RC pupils.

Scotland

Education in Scotland is run by local authorities although school boards, with parent and teacher members, also have a strong say. There are three school categories:

- State schools which are maintained and run by the local education authority.

- Grant aided schools, including those for special educational needs.

- Self-governing schools. Equivalent to grant maintained schools in England.

Phew! Thanks goodness we've got that bit over. Still, the tricky part is in the next chapter......

TOP TIP

Some of this information comes from the DFES and its web site, which is well worth looking into. We recommend that you check out **www.dfs.gov.uk**. Have fun!

CHAPTER 3

Knock, knock! Please let my child in!

We've all heard stories about parents begging, on their hands and knees, for their child to be admitted to the school of their choice. But what exactly are your rights? And – just as important – are there any tips on how to make things swing in your favour?

The basic facts

Your child has the right to a school place between the ages of five and 16. You are entitled to say which school you want your child to go to, even if you're not in the catchment area. But this doesn't guarantee you a place at the school if it's oversubscribed.

The new code

From 2008 (ie applications to start school in September 2008), the new School Admissions Code will hopefully make it fairer for parents to get children in to the school of their choice. Until now, schools are meant to be 'guided' by the code of admission. Now, there will be much clearer guidelines. According to the Department for Education and Skills, the new code should:

● Make sure that schools' admission arrangements and other school policies do not disadvantage children from particular social or racial groups, or those with a disability or special educational needs.

- Prevent any school asking about a parent's financial, marital, work, educational or social status or background.

- Prohibit the use of unfair oversubscription criteria that can discriminate against particular groups. Oversubscription criteria prohibited by the new Code will include:

  - Giving priority to children based solely on whether their parents have made a particular school their first preference. This ends the practice called 'first preference first' which forces many parents to play an 'admissions game' with their children's future, and unnecessarily complicates the admissions system.

  - Stipulating conditions that affect the priority given to an application such as taking account of other schools parents have applied for.

  - Giving priority to children based on their particular interests, specialist knowledge or hobbies.

  - Giving priority to children whose parents are more willing or able to support the school financially.

- Impose a mandatory requirement on admission authorities, schools and Admission Forums to have arrangements in place to cater for children who need a school place outside the normal admission round. This means the most vulnerable children and those whose families move home during the school year, including the children of service personnel, are not disadvantaged. It builds on existing duties to give top priority to children in care and children with statements of special educational needs, even if schools are full.

- Tackle covert selection methods by ensuring other school policies do not discourage parents from applying. For example, it has to set out clear guidelines on choosing a school uniform that is widely available in high street shops and on the internet; and providing school transport for low income families.

- The Code also promotes the practice of giving priority to the younger siblings of children already at primary schools and all secondary schools, including those that select up to 10 per cent of pupils by ability and aptitude – a move which ensures parents can save money on transport and uniforms.

- Schools which use partial selection by ability or aptitude for more than 10 per cent of their intake, and the sibling criteria, have to make sure that their arrangements do not substantially restrict places for other children.

Families who already have children at these schools when the new code comes into force will be unaffected.

How to apply

The local education authority (LEA), or your child's primary school, will provide a form on which you can state your choices. You can put down as many as you want. However, before you do this, ask the LEA for a copy of its rules of admission (also known as admission criteria) as these vary amongst local authorities. For example, some give preference to children who have brothers or sisters already at that school. Some also give priority to parents who make a school their first preference. So if your first choice is a school that's very popular and you are turned down, you may well find that your second and third choices have already been filled by other parents who put them as number one.

Don't assume, either, that because you live near a certain school you are bound to get your child in. Distance from the school might not be on that LEA's criteria for admissions.

The golden rule is not to waste your first choice by selecting a school where you are unlikely to secure a place for your child because the selection criteria are not in your favour.

When to apply

Application forms are usually available from September or October onwards from the previous academic year. But you can still move your child from one school to another outside the usual times. However, you'll need to talk to the relevant local educational authority first.

Which order should you list your choices in

This is a tricky one, isn't it? It's a bit like filling in a lottery ticket. You can't help thinking that if you put down another number instead of the one in your head, you might stand a better chance of winning. Or will you?

The advice we got from teachers and parents alike is to be realistic and, at the same time, to list the school you like best as number one. "There's no point in putting another school that you don't like as much at the top of the list, because you think your child has a better chance of getting in," said a secondary school teacher from York who didn't want to be named. "If you do that, you might always wonder what would have happened if you'd put the school you did like at the top."

Under the new code (see above), you shouldn't be penalised by other schools for putting a certain school at the top. That applies to admissions from 2008. Before then, there is always the possibility this might happen. That's what we mean about being realistic. "I wanted my son to go to a school which had a really good reputation so all the other parents wanted their children to go there," says Sally from London. "We also have another school which isn't quite as good but is still better than the others. Every year, the rumour goes around that if you put down school number one, school number two will turn you down. So we put down school number two for our children. They all got in and we've been very happy there. I think it was worth doing because if we had put down school number one, we might not have got into school number two."

It's also worth talking to other parents who've already been through the system. Find out what they did and what worked for them. So much varies from area to area that it's important to research your local patch.

You could also contact schools directly and ask for advice on listing your choices. They might not give it to you but, on the other hand, you might catch someone unawares and they could let slip some vital information. Do you know any teachers at the school you want your child to go to? Or do you know anyone who does? If so, pump them for inside info. It could be worth it.

Appealing tactics

If, however, your child isn't offered a place at your preferred school, you can appeal. The local education authority will tell you how to do this. Normally, you fill in a form saying you want to appeal and then you are given a date to appear before the panel. At the meeting, the admission authority will explain why it didn't offer you a place. A favourite phrase used to explain this, is that 'the admission would be prejudicial to efficient education or efficient use of resources.' In other words, the school couldn't fit your child in.

If the panel decides there was a good reason for turning down your application, the second stage of the appeal starts. This is where the panel hears your case and why you are appealing.

Here's a checklist of reasons you could give for why your child should go to that school:

- It would suit your child because it offers specialist facilities for, say, music and your child is gifted in this area.

- You already have another child at the school.

- It would be difficult, from a practical point of view, to get your child to another school. For example, you need a school which is close enough for you to pick them up after work. Or you want your child to go to the same school as a brother or sister because it makes transport easier and means you can hand down uniform.

- There are particular medical or social reasons why your child should go to this school.

- Also take reports from teachers at your child's present school which might support your case.

- Contact the PTA and ACE (Advisory Centre for Education) for specific advice on your case.

Extenuating circumstances which you might be able to use include:

- Illness or feeling off colour at the time of taking the examination (if there is one). This will probably only wash if you reported illness at the time to school. You will definitely need a letter from the doctor to confirm this.

- Upsetting circumstances such as divorce, illness, death (including that of a pet) etc which affected examination performance.

- Undetected dyslexia, dyspraxia, difficulty with eye sight and so on which might have affected examinations or general school performance.

If your appeal is successful, the admission authority is legally bound to offer your child a place at the school. If it doesn't, you can ask the school to put your child on their waiting list in case a place becomes free later on.

Finally, if you're unhappy about how the appeal hearing was carried out, you could complain to the Local Government Ombudsman who might recommend a new appeal.

THE EXPERTS SAY...

"I'd recommend that parents attach a letter to their original admissions form, setting out reasons why their child should go to that particular school," says Margaret Morrissey of the PTA. "The form won't tell you to do this but it might help. For example, you could say that you can only get your child to that particular school because it's on your way to work. You could also say that your child knows other children at that school which would be helpful as your child takes time to settle."

To coach or not to coach

This is a very thorny question. It can lead to parents falling out with each other and teachers being cross with parents. But the truth is that many children are coached in order to get into the school of their choice if there's an entrance exam involved.

Tutors don't have to belong to a registered body. So finding a good tutor can be hard. Ask other parents for recommendations and, if you don't think it will annoy them, ask teachers at your child's current school too. The average hourly tuition fee is about £22-£25. Also check out schemes like Kumon for maths and English. These are either held at centres or through private tutors who come to the house.

Useful websites

www.kumon.co.uk
www.personal-tutors.co.uk
www.toptutors.co.uk

Take it from us

"My daughter wrote a letter to the local paper complaining about the lack of bicycle lanes in our town. She was only 10 at the time and thought of the idea herself because we enjoy cycling as a family. The newspaper published it together with a photograph of her. That was about six months before we heard she hadn't got into the school we wanted her to. We took the cutting along to the appeal committee and they decided to accept her because it showed initiative on her part." *Joanne, East Anglia*

"Our dog died during the last year of primary school and it really upset my son. It affected his work and also his 11 plus. I told the committee about it, thinking they'd just dismiss it. But one of the people there was a dog lover and seemed to understand. My son got in." *Maggie, Buckingham*

"It seems to me that appeal committees are full of real people. They do actually listen to the ordinary problems that families have in life. So it's worth telling them about domestic issues, however trivial." *Teacher who didn't want to be named*

"I felt very nervous going into an appeal. But then I told myself I was there for my daughter and not myself. That helped." *Parent who didn't want to be named*

"My son writes lyrics for his guitar. I took some in with me and the committee seemed impressed. He got a place." *Sam, Ealing*

"My daughter has three stepbrothers and we felt it was important for her to go to an all girls school because she was fed up with boys around her all the time. I told the appeals committee that. I don't know if that's what did it, but she got a place." *Jan, Amersham*

"I wanted my daughter to go to a mixed school because I felt disadvantaged at having gone to an all girls school myself. We were offered a place at an all girls school so I appealed and told them about my experience. Did it make a difference? I'm not sure but we got in." *Susie, Norwich*

"I know of friends who didn't appeal because they didn't want to raise their children's hopes or go through what can be a difficult process. We did appeal and although I found it quite humiliating, having to state my case, I feel it was worth it. I also think some of my friends wished they'd done the same. But it was too late." *Ann, London*

CHAPTER 4

It's nearly time to start... how to soothe pre-school nerves

This may sound simple but one of the best ways you can prepare your child for their new school is not to make a fuss about it in the weeks before they start. If you are nervous, they will be too.

You can, however, take some practical measures to reduce the shock of the new. If you're near the new school, you could walk or drive past it. If your child is going to be travelling there alone when term starts, go over the route. Point out where the bus stops. Get your child to do a dry run. Run over what they should do if they miss the bus or you're not there to pick them up.

If you know other children going at the same time, encourage them to come round. Even better, suggest a trip to the cinema or bowling alley. It's less obvious.

Make sure you've got everything ready before the first day. The worst thing for a new kid on the block is to be different and, as parents, we can do our bit. Check they've got the right school uniform and the correct equipment. One of my children recently got a detention for not having a calculator (well, he had been told three times). Don't try to buy new shoes at the last minute and then find no one has your child's size in stock. Label everything and don't do it the night before or your bad mood will infect them.

If your child can't sleep the night before, sit next to them and reassure them. Remind them that all the others will be feeling nervous too. Suggest they find someone who is standing on their own and ask what their name is.

Psychologist and mother Gaynor Sbuttoni adds that it's vital to show your child that you know how they feel. "Don't dismiss those fears by saying 'You'll be all right.' And don't say 'How does it feel?' Instead, try 'I can tell you're feeling really scared about going to school.' Then tell them that most people feel worried, or describe how frightened you were when you first went."

After acknowledging their feelings, we need to change their belief that they can't manage. So we need to get them to close their eyes and imagine that they're going into school on the first day. Ask them to tell you what's the very worst thing that could happen and then what they could do about it. So if the worst thing is not making friends, get them to think of what they'd do. It might be talking to someone on their own. If they really can't think of anything, say 'I had one idea but you might have a better one. How about talking to the person who's in the lunch queue next to you?'

"I was having acupuncture for tennis elbow and my acupuncturist mentioned she'd just treated a teenager for exam stress. I asked if she could help my 11 year old daughter who was very nervous about starting school the following week. Instead of using needles, she massaged her head, temples and shoulders. It really seemed to calm her down."
Marion, London

Bernadette Doherty, headmistress at Wharrier Street Primary

School, Newcastle Upon Tyne, advises, "Get help from your child's primary school. Tell the teachers your child is nervous about starting secondary. They will probably have known your child for some years and might be able to reassure them. Most primary schools have strong links with secondary schools and will have visits both ways. For example, we have secondary school teachers coming to talk to us and we arrange visits to the schools. If your child's school doesn't do that, ask if it can be arranged.

"If your child is going to a new school outside the catchment area, contact the local Educational Welfare Officer. EWOs, as they are known, will arrange visits to the new school and also talk to your child to make them feel more comfortable. Parents can help by spending quiet time talking to their children just as they would helping them to read. Get books from the library too about school life, and talk positively about your own secondary school experiences.

"If they're worried, don't say 'Oh it will be all right.' Allow them to express their fears. Just listening and helping them to let it out will do them good. And try to dispel any myths. There are always a lot of nasty stories going about saying that children at 'big school' will put their heads down the loos. Explain this doesn't happen and if you can, find older children at the school to tell them that."

How do you do?

The big difference for parents when their kids go to secondary school is that there's less contact with other parents and with teachers. There aren't the social opportunities for interaction as there were when you took your little darlings into the classroom or dropped them off in the playground.

This is why it's so important to go to all those parent events outside school. Join the PTA or offer to run the White Elephant stall for the school fete. Do what it takes to get to know the teachers on a friendly level.

Work out a routine

Start as you mean to go on. When your child comes home from school, they'll be tired, hungry and thirsty. Let them rest, but then work out when the best time is to have supper and do homework. What time do you need to get up in the morning to get your child to school? Try to stick to that routine. It's not just reassuring. It also helps to ensure that the work is done and your child goes to bed at a reasonable hour.

School runs

If they can't walk to school, is it worth doing a school run? Before deciding, check you feel confident in the other mothers' driving and reliability. Talk to your children first before setting up a run as they might not get on with the other kids and then refuse to be part of it. Discuss timing and general rules with the others on the run. What do you do if you're running late/someone's sick/someone's left something behind at school and so on? Always make sure you have emergency contact numbers for each other. Ensure everyone will check the kids are strapped in and that you don't have too many in the car, especially if one of them is bringing a friend home for tea.

THE EXPERTS SAY...

"Find out if there are learning mentors," advises Sue Foreman of the National Association of Schoolmasters Union of Women Teachers (NASUWT). "In some schools, there's a scheme where older children help younger ones. In other schools, it's the head of year."

Find out the school rules in advance

Is your child allowed to take in a mobile phone? Or an iPod? If not and your child does this without realising, they might get a detention on day one. Not a great start....

Have a little chat

Sit down when your child is feeling relaxed and gently explain that things will be different when they start at the new school. Warn them that it might feel very strange at first but that they'll get used to it. Remind them that they felt the same way when they started primary school and that they probably got used to that within a few weeks, if not days.

Also flag up possible problem areas without alarming your child. Explain they will have to find their own way from lesson to lesson instead of being in the same classroom. But tell them to latch on to other kids in the class and follow the herd. Also encourage your child to do their best and not mess around. They're old enough, at this stage, to understand that teachers won't know which of the kids are happy to work and which aren't. So if they fool about or talk out of turn to their neighbour, they might be unfairly labelled as a trouble-maker. Sadly, it's very difficult to shake off this label once you've got it.

Ask your child if they've got any questions. You might get a grunt in reply but make it clear that you're there for them if and when they do.

Practical tips

You've probably discovered, like us, that shoes are pretty tricky to label. How anyone can get a pen in that deep to make a name that's recognisable, is beyond us. And even if you achieve it, it gets rubbed out. Those sticker labels don't always stay put either. So try:

- Sewing a name tape, discreetly, round the lace. So it doesn't look too obvious – and become a focus for bullies – cut off the first name and just use the surname.

- Write the name in Tippex on the sole.

- Also Tippex individual pieces of equipment such as calculators, hockey sticks and pens.

- Buy spares of anything that might get lost. In our house, we have spare calculators/school ties (they always seem to be missing on Monday morning) and even an old pair of school shoes.

- When buying a school bag, check that:

- It fits in with school regulations.

- It's as light as possible without any books.

- It distributes the weight evenly across both shoulders.

The problem is that most kids wear theirs, slung across one shoulder which then affects their posture for years to come. So try to get them into a good habit from the beginning. Good luck.

- Keep the receipt. In fact, keep the receipts for everything in a big envelope named EXPENSIVE SCHOOL UNIFORM. Then if the bag's straps do give way owing to the copious number of books inside, you've got some comeback.

- Try and find out beforehand if school provides lockers. Most schools do and this is where kids are meant to keep the books they don't need for the day. In reality, they can't be bothered which means they walk around with all their books in their bag.

- If lockers are provided, your child will probably need to buy a small padlock. These usually come with two sets of keys. Make sure you keep the spare in your possession because we bet you a fiver that your children will have lost theirs by Christmas. Or give them one with a combination, and write down the number somewhere safe.

- Get them a reliable watch with numbers they can easily read. They'll need to learn to be in certain places at certain times so they don't stand a chance without one. Scratch their name on the back. That way, it's less likely to get nicked than if you put an adhesive name label on it.

- Get them to sharpen pencils and pack their bag before the big day.

- Slip one of your business cards and/or address details inside their jacket pocket or school bag so they know they can contact you.

- Make sure they've got enough money for school lunch/emergency transport home.

- If they don't have a mobile phone, get them a phone card.

- Work out an emergency procedure in case they get home and can't get in or if you're not there to pick them up.

Show this one to your kids

Here are some valuable safety tips for going to school, from

Kidscape, the charity which helps children to protect themselves.

- Avoid taking short cuts through dark or deserted places.

- Never hitchhike or take rides from strangers, and try to avoid walking home alone.

- If someone approaches you asking directions, keep your distance or walk away and pretend not to hear.

- If you are threatened, yell and run away, if possible.

- If you are being followed, go into a shop or towards people.

- Try crossing the road to see if the person follows.

- Do not wear an iPod\mp3 player/personal stereo as it prevents you being aware of what is happening around you.

- Keep your mobile hidden when you're not using it.

- Think twice about getting the latest phone model – expensive handsets could attract potential thieves and muggers.

- Avoid empty carriages on trains.

- On buses or the underground, sit near the driver or guard.

- If you are attacked, think of what you might do. Would you talk your way out of it or pretend to do what you are asked, while waiting for a chance to get away? Only you can decide what to do in the event.

- If you do have to defend yourself, take a deep breath and try not to panic. Use anything you have to hand to defend yourself – keys, an umbrella, the heel of your shoe, hairspray.

- Remember that anything you do or any item you use is to provide you with an opportunity to get away. Unless you are trained in self-defence, it is absolutely senseless to stay around.

- If you are faced with a knife or another weapon, probably your best defence is to remain calm and give the attacker whatever possessions he or she demands. If they are going to assault you, you might try to talk your way out. Whatever you do, it must be your decision.

Getting away strategies to practise

- If someone grabs your arms with their hands, jerk your arm away in the direction of the attacker's thumb – this is the weakest part of anyone's grip.

- If someone grabs you from behind, bend forward and come back quickly, slamming your head against their face or chin (the back of your head is very hard, but it may hurt you as well).

- If they have a weapon and you think you have a chance to do something to get away, scrape your heel down the inside of the attacker's leg, or kick them in the knee hard. Then stamp on their instep with all your weight. Then run in the direction of shops or people.

- Kicking someone in the genitals or poking them in the eyes is not as easy as you might have heard. If you kick up at an attacker, they may just grab your leg and you will end up on the ground.

- Only ever try something you feel confident you can complete, or you might just do enough to make the attacker even angrier.

THE EXPERTS SAY...

Here are some more tips for getting your child settled, this time from Heather Summers, neurolinguistic expert and mother:

- If possible, involve your child when choosing the school.

- Go round the school more than once if possible. Meet the teachers.

- Make sure they are with a group of good friends all of whom are going to the same school. (Foster the friendships in advance if necessary.)

- Gather the help of an older sibling or pupil you know and trust who is already at the school and ask them to be a mentor/buddy to your child. Have a three way meeting in advance of the child going to school and get the chosen person to say what they will be doing to help.

- Get as much information as possible from those people you know who already go to the school, and find ways to get them to share that information with your child.

- Use positive language such as '...going to Secondary School now you are growing up', painting positive pictures of the school in terms of what it will offer.

- If your child is reluctant to go to secondary school and is not keen on change, point out all the things in the new school that are the same or similar to the one they are leaving. 'Just think, going to secondary school will be very similar to your primary school. You'll have many of the same friends, you'll still be able to do your favourite activities (art, music, maths) and learn even more about them, you've met some of the teachers and they seem to be just as nice as the ones in your current school, don't they?'

If the child likes change and difference then point out all the things that will be new, exciting and changed in secondary school, for example, 'Your new school will be very different to your old one. You'll have a different teacher for each subject, you'll be able to make many new friends, you'll have different sports and subjects such as French/chemistry/netball which you didn't have before'.

TOP TIP

A recent survey from Parentline Plus showed what parents are most worried about when their children start secondary school:

53 per cent worry about children getting bullied

20 per cent worry about drinking/drugs/smoking

17 per cent worry about whether their child will be happy there

15 per cent worry about their child making friends

13 per cent worry about peer pressure

13 per cent worry about their child getting in with the wrong crowd

11 per cent worry whether the child will do well academically

---

CHAPTER 5

The first week at school

Sweaty, nervous, worried about not being able to give the right answers, terrified of not finding a friend... And that's just how you feel as a parent. So imagine how it feels for them.

Avoid pre-school panics

A few days before – preferably not the night before or you'll worry them even more – go over the routine you need to follow in order to get them to school on time. Try to get them to bed on time so they're not too exhausted the next day. But don't overdo it. If you make them have a really early night, they won't be sleepy and then they'll toss and turn with apprehension. Explain when they need to get up in the morning and build in an extra five to 10 minutes leeway.

Try these tactics too:

- If you've got other children, you might need to get them up earlier too to accommodate the new routine.

- Put out the new school uniform the night before so they know where it is. That way, they can get themselves dressed without asking you where their stuff is.

- Make sure their school bag is already packed with essentials like pencil case and calculator etc. Do they have money for lunch if they need it?

- If they're not hungry, don't force them to eat breakfast. Yes of course it's the most important meal of the day but they might be feeling sick with nerves. If you don't make a fuss now, they'll be more inclined to be relaxed the next day and then they will eat something. Instead, suggest they take a banana which has slow releasing energy.

- If you're not taking them to school, try to make sure they go with someone else on the first day. You'll need to have organised this before hand. It might be another child starting at the same time or an older one who lives nearby.

THE EXPERTS SAY...

"First impressions count. Tell your child it's important not to mess around but to listen carefully in class, get homework in on time and be organised. Get them to pack their bag the night before. At first, you can check they've done their homework by looking in their homework diaries but at the end of the day, you have to leave them to their own devices. It would be good if parents could back teachers up by explaining that education is important even if they don't like some of the other children or teachers. We need children to come to school with the idea that learning is a good thing. Hitting the internet button is not enough. So many kids see people becoming celebrities overnight on television that they think they can do the same. Parents and teachers need to explain that success usually comes from hard work." *Mandy Haehner, London teacher and spokesman for the National Association of School Masters Union of Women Teachers*

"Now are you sure you've got everything? Car keys? Handkerchief?
Know the directions...?"

Take it from us

"My daughter is terrible at getting up on time. So I bought
three alarm clocks and set them off at five minute intervals."
Ann, Southampton

"I set all the clocks five minutes fast. Although they might twig
before long, it's amazing how you can still look at a clock and
think 'Help, I've got to dash.'" *Jane, Hertfordshire*

"Make sure they know how to contact you if you're not going to be at home. Although the school will have your details, your child might need to get hold of you urgently. Put your mobile number on their phone or on a piece of paper in their pocket." *Michael, Brighton*

"My daughter used to spend ages on the loo when it was time to go to school. With hindsight, it was because she was nervous but I used to get really uptight because it made us late for school. In the end, I had to get her up 10 minutes earlier to build in time." *Katy, Chichester*

How was it for you?

There you are, on tenterhooks, desperate to know how he got on with his first day. And there he is, kicking off his shoes, flinging his tie to the ground and marching up to his bedroom to log onto MSN.

Kids need time to chill out. Some need longer than others. You're more likely to pry out information if you wait until the time is right and they're ready to talk to you. This might be over tea or it could be when they're just about to fall asleep. So sit tight.

You can, however, like all good interrogators, ask leading questions. Try to make these the kind that require a proper answer instead of a 'yes' or 'no' as you'll learn more. For example, instead of asking if they made any friends, ask where his new friends live and where they went to school before.

Ideally, if you can, have tea ready in case they're starving. Remember how hungry we felt at the end of the school day? It's also a good idea to have food that can wait if they're not hungry and also food that they really like. This might sound old-fashioned, as though we're pandering to them, but they've just been through one of the most traumatic experiences of their life. They deserve to be pampered. After all, when they've got into the swing of things, you can go back to being a dragon.

Kick that routine into action

Remember we talked about working out a routine when they start secondary school? When they were babies, they were comforted by a routine, weren't they? And it also provided a comforting structure for you too.

Well, things haven't changed. If you can get your secondary school child into some kind of pattern now, you'll stand a better chance later on of making sure that they do their homework and coursework on time and still be able to chill out.

The right kind of routine will depend very much on the kind of child you have. There's more on this in the next chapter, on homework.

Now they're talking

At some point, either at the end of the first day or part of the way through the week, they probably will start to open up and tell you about their first week. Then you'll probably wish you'd never asked. So what do you do if they say…

'I hate it!'

Understanding what they're going through will help a lot, even though they may not show their emotions. Think how you feel if you're crying on someone's shoulder about something and they say 'That must be very hard'. They're not solving the problem – which might be insoluble anyway – but it's reassuring to have that understanding and recognition that you're going through a difficult time.

So if they come back from their new school and declare that they hate it, listen to why they dislike it so much. Make them a cup of tea or whatever soothes them. And then gently suggest that they might feel differently the next day or the next week when it's not all so strange. Remind them of other times when they started something new and didn't like it. They might have forgotten how long it took to accept their earlier school, or scouts, or even moving house.

Try to pin them down on why they hate it so much. Is it because they haven't made friends? Did the maths teacher give them a detention? Was lunch disgusting? Could they do the work? Then try to help your child work out a strategy on how to cope with each one. If possible, try to do so without contacting school. It's easy to get a reputation as an overprotective parent if you start ringing up from day one. If you know another more established parent at the school whose child has been there for a year or more, ring and ask what they would do. I did this with a friend for some years. And now another new parent is doing the same with me. It's what we call parent support links and it might well involve a cup of coffee or something stronger along the way. If you can't sort it out after that, consider ringing the year head.

'I don't have any friends'

It's difficult for a child to go to a school if their old friends have gone somewhere else. (See earlier chapters on choosing a school and why it can be helpful for your child to go to the same one as their mates.) But sometimes it can't be helped.

Kids can be very fickle when it comes to friendships. Your child and their best friend might have been thick as thieves at primary school. But the so-called best friend might well find another mate at secondary school, especially if they're in a different set or class. It makes your heart bleed for them, doesn't it? You can, however, teach them some strategies for making new friends. Try these:

- Get them to ask the child sitting nearest them what their name is, where they live, what they think of the teacher, whether they play football, if they go on My Space and so on.

- Suggest that if the kid next to them loses their pen, rubber or whatever, your child lends them a spare (which you, of course, will have put in their school bag).

- Encourage them to join after-school clubs like football, drama or music. They might meet more like-minded souls than the swot sitting next to them in maths.

- Also encourage them to befriend anyone who's standing on their own. Remind them that that kid is probably feeling awkward too.

- If someone joins the school a few weeks or months after everyone else, try and persuade your child to say hello. Remind them how they felt at the start of the new term. Point out that the 'new kid' might be a good friend in waiting.

THE EXPERTS SAY...

"Why don't they have friends? Listen to why they think they don't have them and suggest they join after-school clubs or something outside school." *Professor Cary Cooper*

'I hate the maths teacher'

Why is it always maths? (Seriously, it could easily be another subject.) The sad fact is that although we expect teachers to be adults, some aren't always as good at dealing with children as we'd like. And children certainly aren't always as good at dealing with teachers as we'd like. The result can be a very difficult head-on which can have repercussions for years to come.

Now you've hopefully already had that little pep talk with your child before he started. You've pointed out that it's important to be polite to teachers and not, as my son's head of year is always suggesting, to put their head 'above the parapet'. In other words, you've told them that it's pretty crucial to keep their nose clean and toe-lick if necessary.

But they haven't listened. Literally. They've asked the maths teacher something which she told them a few minutes earlier and now she's cross your child didn't pay more attention. Or maybe she's just having a bad day and is being unnecessarily tough. Perhaps she's a lousy teacher and can't put the facts across.

Either way, they haven't hit it off and now your child is in danger of loathing maths and, in your imagination at least, struggling when it comes to GCSEs. So what do you do?

- Ask your child what they'd do if they'd just started work and had a difficult boss. Walk out? No, or they wouldn't get paid.

- Suggest that it might be a good idea to show the boss that you've turned over a new leaf. Recognise where you went wrong, such as not listening to instructions. And from that day onwards, make sure you do listen.

- Be polite. Don't gossip with your colleagues about what a lousy boss they are. In other words, don't whisper to the kid who's sitting next to you that you think she's a word we can't print on this page.

- Talking about writing on pages, explain that it really isn't a good idea to write 'I hate Miss X' on your maths book or homework diary. Although the homework diary is meant to be a child's own personal record of what they've got to do for homework, it is generally used by any self-respecting kid as an illustration pad for rude words and comments about other kids and teachers. Unfortunately, teachers are well aware of this and often swoop down in spot reading checks.

'The loos are disgusting'

This isn't as funny as it sounds. When one of my children started secondary school, he (and I) were appalled to find that the locks on the doors were always being vandalised. No sooner did school repair them than they were broken again. I wish now that I'd made a fuss because he, understandably, found it very difficult to sit in peace without fear of someone bursting through the door. So take these comments seriously. This really is one for the year head.

'The food is gross'

Bet it's not as bad as our food was when we were at school... Still, nowadays there's no excuse for substandard food. Of course, it might just be that your child is fussy. Even so, we all need to eat in order to work. So if your child really hates lunch, ask if he can take a packed lunch in or give him nutritious snacks that he can eat at the same time.

'The work's too difficult'

If they'll let you, sit down and go through the work that they find tricky. It might be that it's not too different from their previous school's curriculum but that questions are phrased in another way. Try to help them unravel this.

If this doesn't work, and you have an older child on the

premises, rope them in too. Younger kids sometimes respond better to under 25 year olds. My eldest son has always been brilliant at helping his younger brother in a way that my youngest wouldn't take from me.

If the work is really that different, give it a few days to see if things improve and then, if they don't, see the year head. Tactfully point out that your child was using different methods beforehand and is having trouble now. Also see Chapter Eighteen on dealing with difficult teachers.

At the end of the day

Work out an evening routine. This applies to every day but if you make a point of doing it during the first week, it will become a habit. Yes, of course it's difficult if you're working, have other children, have a partner who comes in late, or have no partner at all. But in the long term, it's worth it. Here are some examples.

- Have a set bath and bedtime and stick to it. Don't let them push you into extending the deadline because there's something on television or they're still talking to friends on MSN.

- Allow a winding down time between homework and bed.

- Oversee the 'packing of the school bag'. Don't underestimate the importance of this. Never, ever let them do it the following morning or you'll add to the pre-school panic.

- Go through their homework diary. This is where they are meant to have made a note of what homework has to be done when. Have they done everything they should have done? Ignore the rude pictures.

- Get them to put their dirty clothes in the linen bin (see *Tidy*

Your Room, also White Ladder Press, £7.99). Get them to help you put out clean underwear and school uniform for the next day.

● Encourage them to read in bed. I always say I don't care what my kids read as long as they are reading. Now my son is 15, his 'magazines' aren't exactly what I had in mind for reading matter but I comfort myself with the thought that there are some words on the page as well as pictures.

Take it from us

"If you say you're going to be home when your child gets back from school, make sure you are – or that someone else is. In the early days of starting school, they need that security. Don't assume that because they're old enough to go to secondary school, they're old enough to cope with an empty house. We all like someone to talk to at the end of the day. If you or someone else can't be there, arrange an alternative. Maybe your child can go to a neighbour or friend." *Isobel, Cardiff*

"Go over house rules. As your child gets older, they may well find themselves coming back to an empty house. But that doesn't mean they can start frying chips or having a house party." *Adrienne, Pinner*

"When my son started secondary school, we agreed he would come straight back home every evening. But one night, he was an hour late and I was beside myself. He'd decided to go back to a new friend's house and hadn't phoned me. I couldn't believe he had broken the rule we had made. But the excitement of having more freedom at a secondary school can sometimes go to their heads." *Andy, Manchester*

"In Year 7, help your child be organised before they start secondary. Go over the bus routes with them so they're not terrified on the first day, or find a local helpful teenager to keep an eye for the first few days. Make sure they have a cheap phone (so they don't get mugged, but can contact you when they've missed the bus or left their bag at the bus stop as has happened to me). Do contact the school if you're worried, it's very intimidating but you know your child better then they do."

"As a teacher, I am often amazed by how worried children get and don't tell me, so I really encourage parents to contact me for the slightest thing. Boys hate 'snitching'." *Caroline, teacher and parent, Amersham*

THE EXPERTS SAY...

"The key point is to talk, and listen, to your child. They will feel excitement, nerves, anticipation and trepidation at various times, and these will be highlighted as the new term approaches. Support and encourage your child – show interest without being intrusive. Parent-offspring relationships come under strain in the adolescent years, but this is when your growing teenager needs parent and school to provide opportunities, to encourage participation and to impose realistic limits on behaviour.

"Secondary education expands the students' horizons – each youngster will handle the expansion in a different way. Schools and parents can support the student as he/she exploits the opportunities available, and it is important for both to work together in the interests of the student.

"Listen to your child, praise their achievements, but make it clear when they have gone outside acceptable limits. Also, make it clear that you will always be there for them, even if you do not necessarily approve of everything they do." *Jeff Holman, father and assistant secretary of the National Association of Head Teachers (NAHT)*

"Going to secondary school is a time of great change in a family's life, together with all the worry and excitement of becoming a teenager. Now children have to face going from being the oldest at primary school to being the youngest in a huge school.

"There are lots of new things to get used to, including the amount of homework which can really seem to multiply. Help your children to take responsibility for organising and doing their homework and never forget to praise them for their hard work. Many schools have a homework diary, or daybook for parents to sign each day. This helps you and your child know that their homework is being monitored.

"The amount of stuff your child will need to take to school can seem enormous so encourage them to be organised and set out everything they need the night before so there isn't a huge panic in the morning with everyone's nerves being frayed.

"Find out more about the school's meetings with parents and if there is a PTA and make a point of signing the home school agreement and use the opportunity to ask any questions you have about the new school.

"Encourage your child to talk to you about anything that is worrying them and if something does come up, talk to your child's class teacher. Many secondary schools now have a member of staff with particular responsibility for pastoral issues and there should be an opportunity for you to talk in confidence about anything that might be worrying your child. This could include worries about bullying, personality clashes with teachers or concerns about schoolwork.

"As a parent, ensure you look after yourself and your family too. It's a time of life change and it is all right to feel loss and sadness as your child begins to grow up and find independence, making choices without you." *Parentline Plus*

CHAPTER 6

Have you done your homework?

When I got married, a well meaning, much married uncle advised me to start as I meant to go on. Well forget that – marriage is another book, or maybe even a tome. But it sure as heck applies to homework.

Routine, routine, routine

That's what you have to establish from the very first day when your child comes home, announcing they have homework to do. We've mentioned this briefly before but we're going to do so again because it's so important. Believe me. I've been there with three different children, all of whom have done it in different ways, with varying amounts of enthusiasm and success.

If your child knows when they have to do their homework, you're halfway there. Why? Because when one of their mates (who should be doing their own prep) rings to ask them out to play/hang around town, you can say with authority that it's 'homework time'.

Now I know this won't hold much water when your offspring get older. (Don't worry. We've got some advice for that tricky period a bit later in the chapter.) But in Year 7 your children will hopefully still be at the stage where they'll accept the existence of homework time and respect it.

There are, however, certain factors to consider before establishing when is the best time to start homework. No self-respecting child will want to open their geography book if their favourite programme is on telly. And no child – or adult – can concentrate if they're hungry or thirsty. Similarly, they can't give homework their best chance if they are tired. So you need to make sure that homework time is not too early or too late.

We can't tell you that 6pm is the best time to start. You need to take your own family needs and considerations into account. You may also need to make some adjustments along the way. But try to find a pattern as soon as possible. It will stand you both in good stead in the long run.

Break it up

Kids, like adults, work in different ways. Some like to get it all done in one go. Others need a breather. Sometimes, if your child is like one of mine (whom I won't name), they need a very long breather. In fact, so long they forget they ought to go back to their homework at all.

You know your child best. So give them guidance. If they do have breaks, agree a certain time. Set it by their watch and or the computer clock.

Homework on the computer

Yes, I know. Computers have revolutionised our lives. But there are times when I wish they hadn't been invented until, at least, my youngest had safely finished his secondary school career. In our house MSN, or Instant Messengering as it is known, is the biggest threat to homework since The Simpsons.

The problem with computers is that most schools encourage them. Pupils are taught to look up information online and many need a computer in order to do their homework and/or course-work.

The problem with our kids is that they are very good at pretending to do their homework while, in reality, they are chatting to their friends online. I can't be the only parent who walks into their child's bedroom only to hear the telltale pinging when they swiftly switch from MSN to the thrills of stalactites and stalagmites.

There are various tactics we can follow to beat this computer v homework battle. Here are some of them. But they come with a parental warning. They'll only work if your child is willing to compromise. If not, there's very little you can do about it apart from wait until the end of term report. If it says they haven't done their homework, or have done it inadequately, you might think of confiscating the computer altogether. Tough words. But it's a tough world out there.

- Strike a deal. Your child promises not to go on MSN/My Space etc while they're doing their homework. If they break the promise, reduce the time they're allowed on the computer for fun.

- Ban computer-for-fun time until homework is completed.

- Allow it only during homework breaks.

- Take the computer away – easier if it's a laptop. The length of time you do this for depends on the severity of the problem.

- Ideally, don't have the computer in your child's room. It's easier to monitor if it's in a family space.

- If this is difficult, try and remove it before bedtime. I started doing this when I found my son would get out of bed and start chatting to friends when I thought he was asleep.

- Show your children you appreciate the computer's importance in their lives. Get them to demonstrate how certain things work to make them feel good about themselves. Don't get us wrong. Computers can be great when they're used correctly. But they can also be addictive and, as such, interfere with homework.

Are they sitting comfortably?

Another key to successful homework practice is to provide a quiet, cosy place for your child where they feel comfortable. It doesn't matter if they don't have their own bedroom. A private corner can be anywhere the television isn't blaring and other children aren't distracting them. Also try these ideas:

- Setting up a study corner can be a useful way of getting them interested in homework. Maybe you could choose a desk together if they haven't got one already. It doesn't have to be expensive. There are plenty of flat-packs around or you could have a rummage round a secondhand shop. My sister still has the Edwardian desk which my mother found in Mrs Mogg's shop in Harrow and which she sanded down and rewaxed.

- Make or buy a pencil container and sharpen pencils as a 'starter' present. After that, they can do it themselves. Have a spare supply of rubbers, rulers and geometrical sets because you can bet your bottom dollar that one night they'll forget to bring them back home.

- Check the chair is at the right height to the desk and is suitable for the size of your child. If they're wriggling uncomfortably, they're less likely to get work done.

- Is the lighting adequate? You might need to buy an extra desk light. Again, this doesn't have to be expensive.

● Is the room warm enough? Maybe they need another jumper or an extra heater.

Do not disturb

You know what it's like when someone interrupts you in the middle of work or when you're reading a good book. Well kids don't like being interrupted either. Fair enough if they're doing something they shouldn't. But if you're always checking up on them when they're working, you'll distract them and defeat the object. On the other hand, you might want to make sure they're doing what they say they are...

Short of installing a security camera, you might have to trust them on this one. I do know of parents who listen at the door for the ping pong of MSN (OK, I admit it) but there comes a time when you have to let them get on with it. If they get into trouble for not doing their homework, they'll hopefully learn to be more responsible next time.

'I can't remember what I've got for homework'

How often have you heard that one? Of course, they should have written it down in their homework diary. And no doubt, you'll point this out. But it won't solve the immediate problem.

So what will? Suggest your child rings someone else in their class or set to find out what homework was given. While everyone's new they might not have the phone number, but maybe they can email. Can you ring another parent? It's probably wise to check this out with your child first as they might not want you to do this.

If all else fails, send a note into school explaining that unfortunately your child wasn't sure what to do for homework. It's best to do this rather than let it go as the teacher might think your child hasn't bothered. That's how bad reputations begin.

When your child sets off for school the next day, remind them to write down their homework so they don't forget that day. This might sound like being fussy but remember this is still new for your kids.

'I can't do it!'

It's not always easy for children to cope with the homework load at secondary school. They might not have got very much at primary – and the level will have been very different. Most secondary school teachers are aware of this but it's still important for children to establish good practices.

They will do this if you're encouraging. So if they come back and say 'I've got loads of homework tonight', don't join in their groans. Be positive and they'll be more positive too.

If they genuinely can't do their homework, don't immediately rush in and do it for them. You might get them a bad mark anyway (one of my sons still blames me for a C minus in Year 11). And as for maths, don't touch it unless you're an expert. They do it differently nowadays and you'll immediately be rumbled.

A friend of mine has a panel of other friends who are specialists in certain areas including maths, geography and French. When her daughter is stuck, she rings them up. But guess what? When it came to exam time, her daughter did dismally…

There are also certain websites which will translate French/German/Spanish/Latin texts and also provide already written essays. If you catch your children doing this, point out that it won't help them in the long run. Then have a private moan about why they didn't have them in our day…

Seriously, if your child really can't do their homework, there's only one way out of it. Either you or they have to see the teacher. A good one won't get cross but will explain how to do it. If your child says the teacher wouldn't or couldn't do this, take the matter to the year head. Sadly, some teachers can't teach. But there's no reason why our children should suffer for it.

'I forgot to hand my homework in'

I've lost count of the number of times I've heard this said. And I'm afraid there are no magic wands to wave. Your child simply has to learn to remember. It's part of getting to grips with a new routine.

You can, however, give little reminders. I know mums who:

● Put stickers on their child's homework diary to remind them to hand in homework.

● Send reminder text messages to their child's mobile phone.

● Have faxed 'left behind homework' through to the school office.

But where do you stop? In the end, they have to learn for themselves.

'I haven't finished'

If it's bedtime and your child is still working, encourage them to call it a day. It's difficult for most people to work well at that time of night and they'll be exhausted the next day. If it simply has to be in by tomorrow, suggest they get up earlier to finish it.

'There's too much'

You're more likely to encounter this problem as your child gets older. My lot always used to complain that the teachers never knew how much the other teachers were setting with the result that they had too much homework in too short a term.

Certainly this can happen. If it does, suggest to your child that they ask their year head for advice. It might be that teachers need to communicate more.

'I want to go out with my mates instead of doing homework'

This is where the routine bit comes in handy. Establish a rule that they don't go out during the week until homework is done. Of course, the temptation then is to rush it, so you might want to take a look and check it's all done. As your child gets older you won't be able to do this, but you can try and teach the basic principles as soon as possible.

Either that or ban going out with friends during the week altogether. In some ways, it's the easier option even though you won't be very popular.

'My teacher marked my homework unfairly'

Are you sure? Before you go marching in to school demanding a remark, take a look. Maybe this is a subject that's better raised at a parents' evening (see Chapter Twenty Two) than in the early days when you might create a bad reputation for yourself.

On the other hand, I have been known – much to my children's horror – to correct ungrammatical comments made by certain teachers over the years in my children's books. I don't advise this as it doesn't go down well. But I just couldn't stop myself…

Holidays and school projects

Homework is the last thing they want to do on holiday. But if you can encourage them to do some extra reading or look up old notes, it will set them up for the next term. Use holidays to get them interested in a subject. There are some great hands-on museums like Eureka in Halifax, West Yorkshire.

Take it from us

"My daughter has a chart, written in her diary, listing the subjects she has to do homework for. In her homework diary she's meant to write down when it has to be handed in. I've encouraged her to make a wall chart and write it all down." *Mel, Essex*

"My son found it hard to organise homework at first, especially if he had a few days to do a piece of work. He'd always leave it to the last minute or forget it. I suggested he did it that night so it was done and dusted. I pointed out it would give him more time to do what he wanted to do when everyone else was still working. It took a few weeks to persuade him but now he's always first to hand it in." *Jane, Southampton*

"There wasn't anywhere quiet for me to work at home so I went to the library or the local youth centre. It was fine there. Nice and warm too." *Tom, 15, London*

How much homework should they be doing at this age?

Here's the recommended amount of homework according to **www.homeworkhigh.com**:

Years 7 and 8	45 minutes to 90 minutes a day
Year 9	1 to 2 hours
Years 10 and 11	$1^1/2$ to $2^1/2$ hours a day
Years 12 to 13	This will depend on workload

CHAPTER 7

Teach them to be organised

One of the best ways you can help your child succeed at school is to teach them to be organised. We can't stress how important this is. In fact, it's one of the main differences between primary school and secondary school. Children are expected to learn to think for themselves from day one at 'big' school. But sometimes they need a helping hand.

"At primary school, everything is done for them," points out Professor Cary Cooper, psychologist and father. "At secondary, no one does much and they're expected to know what's what. They need parents to help kick-start them into organising themselves. So when they start, sit down and write out a contract. Tell them that if they need taking to places, you need notice. When they come back from school, they need to be encouraged to put their school uniform away in a place where they will find it the next morning. The same goes for text books. They should also write a list of things they need for the next day or get their bag ready the night before. Suggest they keep a separate diary from their homework diary and write down when essays are due in. They could also do the same on the computer."

Packing their bag

Again, we've touched on this one but it's essential to make sure they've got everything in it for the next day. A simple 'Have you got everything?' isn't always enough if your child isn't used to gathering up all the text books and other stuff they'll need for lessons. I know this sounds as though you're being overprotective but it can really help if you read out the subjects for the following day and get your child to make sure they've got the right stuff in their bag.

After a few days, your child should get into the habit of doing this themselves. If they don't, and forget stuff, they'll soon get detentions. Then it's up to them to sort the problem out. There's only so much you can do for them or else they won't learn. On the other hand, if your child continues to get told off for forgetting stuff, you might need to do the odd 'booster', giving them a checklist or reminding them when they need to remember something essential.

Go through their school bag for missing school notes

This is an essential piece of advice for all first time parents of kids at secondary schools. Every Friday night, at least, tip their bag onto the floor. You'll need to vacuum up the crumbs and other unmentionables that also fall out, but we guarantee it will be worth it. Amongst that rubbish is bound to be at least one crucial school note about parents' evening, a change of term dates or details of the class trip to Whipsnade which has to be signed by yesterday.

> **TOP TIP**
>
> Use this as a way of finding out more about your child. A receipt, eh? So that's what he bought at Tesco when you thought he'd just gone in for a snack.

Sports kit

This has always been a thorny problem in our house. It's amazing how one sports sock can go missing on the days when someone has to take their sports kit in. The trick is to teach your child to pack it the night before and make sure everything is there. Unfortunately, this is one area where you do have to get involved unless you've persuaded your kids to do the laundry too.

Try also to get them into the habit of bringing their sports kit back with them after games. Again, I've lost count of the number of times my son hasn't got his because he's left it at school and now can't find it. Nag and cajole them into looking through the lost property box. If they won't, or don't find the missing items, you might have to go down yourself. The lost property box, by the way, sorts out the Parents Who Label Carefully from the Parents Who Don't.

Here are a couple more points about keeping the sports kit in the right place at the right time:

- Don't be surprised if your child comes back with a sports top that bears someone else's label. It seems to be the norm for them to pick up the nearest jogging top or track suit bottom that they can find, regardless of whose name they have on it. If the item is of a superior quality to the one you sent your child off in, you might feel less inclined to get them to find the genuine article. But if not, you might need to get them to do something about it.

- In general, don't expect the sports staff to get involved in finding missing garments. They're too busy doing their real jobs. You could try writing a letter but it might not get you very far.

What, where and when

Get your child to draw a large, colourful chart for their bedroom wall, stating which subjects they have on which days. This will become particularly useful when they have coursework which has to be handed in at different times.

Also make a copy for yourself. Yes, of course they should learn to take responsibility for themselves. But a little bit of nagging does-n't always go amiss. Then you can point out that it's Tuesday, isn't it, so shouldn't he have his maths project ready?

"Didn't you notice when you put it on that it wasn't yours?"

Exam timetable

So they've got exams coming up? Then somewhere in their bag or homework diary they should have a copy of their exam timetable. Get them to find it and if they can't, to get it off a friend. Encourage them to pin it on their wall so they know which exam they've got and when. See also Chapter Twenty One on exams and revision.

Write dates down in your diary

This bit of organisational skill is down to you, I'm afraid. Most schools have a list of dates for future events such as the end of term, parents' evening, school fete and so on. The list tends to be sent out with reports and other stuff so you might well be tempted to put it to one side, intending to write it down in your diary or on the calendar. And then you forget.

Over the years, I've learned that it's much better to write it all down immediately. Then you can feel smug when other parents ring you in a panic to check dates.

"I began writing dates down when my son came back from school in floods of tears. It had been a no-school-uniform day and everyone else was in casual clothing. Because I hadn't written down the date, my son was the odd one out. He'd tried to ring me to bring in his ordinary clothes but couldn't get hold of me at work. I felt dreadful because I remembered how it felt to be different. But it wasn't as bad as a friend of mine who got the first day of term wrong. She dropped her daughter off at the school gates, thinking it was quiet because she was early, and then went to London for the day. Her 12 year old daughter was pretty upset." Sue, Southend

I can't find my homework

Well, that's because your room is in a mess, isn't it? Once a month, if you've got that sort of child, get them to sort out their school books and put them into piles. My son has a pile for maths, another for geography and so on. This is a fairly new innovation because he kept losing homework. So in desperation I encouraged him to put everything into groups on his desk and floor. It really has helped.

"When my son has done one piece of work, I get him to put it straight into his school bag so it's ready to take into school the next day. Before that, he'd put it on the desk or floor and then forget to pack it." Jill, Derbyshire

Where's my tie?

Why are we meant to know? It's not as though we have to wear school uniform. Now if your child was organised and put their clothes away the night before, we wouldn't have that problem, would we? Easier said than done. The only real answer, in my experience, is to nag them until they finally get the habit of putting their clothes on a chair or somewhere allocated for the purpose.

Another tip is to hang the offending tie on a coat hanger with the shirt and blazer. Or put the hair scrunchie on the hanger with the dress or skirt. Gloves should automatically go into pockets. And clean socks can be put out the night before, tucked into school shoes.

Ideally, of course, they should do this themselves. But you might just need to check. Otherwise, the pre-school panic will be even worse than usual. And not only is that bad for you, but it also gets them off to a bad start.

"I used to constantly go on at my daughter because she was disorganised. But then I realised she was dyslexic. I would always advise parents to check this out if their children are constantly forgetting things or not able to file things properly." June, York

CHAPTER 8

Friends

Will they make friends at their new 'big' school? This is going to be a major point at the top of your worry list – and theirs too. In fact, this is one of the scariest things about starting a new school, especially if their old friends aren't going to be with them.

We've already given you some guidance in Chapters Three and Four, but if your child still hasn't made any friends by the end of the third or fourth week, you might need to give them a helping hand. Is there another child who lives near you who's in their year? If so, could you ask them and their parents round for an informal coffee?

Can you suggest your children join an after-school club where there'll be others from the same class or year? Sometimes kids get on better in a non-academic environment.

Keep boosting their confidence. Tell them how good they are at something. A child will find it easier to make friends if they feel good about themselves.

Call these friends? Well I don't like them...

So, your child has made friends but you don't think much of them. They eat with their mouths open, they mumble instead of talking, they don't take their shoes off and they fail to say please or thank you.

And it could get worse. They might have earrings in every visible orifice. They could have parents who don't seem to care. And they might... well, let's just stop there.

There's a golden rule when it comes to all your children's friends. And that's to make them feel welcome, even though you'd rather they were at the other end of town instead of in your house. Ask them if they'd like to stay for pizza. Admire their earrings and ask where they had their ears pierced. Win their confidence. Don't, whatever you do, tell your child you don't like them. You never know, you might genuinely find that underneath those earrings/heavy make up, they're really nice.

There is, however, an exception. If you are really worried that your child has fallen into a bad crowd that's doing something illegal, talk to your child and point out the dangers. Ask them what they like about their new friends. Explain that some friends might seem nice but can in fact be dangerous. Now you might not get anywhere with this line of approach. But if you've raised the subject in a non-aggressive and non-argumentative way, your children will hopefully feel able to talk to you if the friendship goes wrong.

If you're seriously concerned about the effect of these friends on your child, you could talk to other parents. Gently try to find out whether this gang is a genuine bad lot or whether they just look that way.

And if you feel your child's new friends are affecting their school progress, you could take a gamble and share your concerns with the class teacher or year head. You would have to ask them to keep this confidential but, even so, there is the danger that your interference might leak back to your child. It's your call whether this is worth it. On the other hand, it might alert the teacher to something that they haven't noticed and prompt them to separate the troublemakers from each other and your child.

This is a tricky issue and one that's difficult to give firm guidelines on since every situation is different. But be on the watch.

Take it from us

"I was worried about my daughter's friends so I asked a friend's older daughter what she thought of them (she was at the same school). She thought they seemed all right so I trusted her judgement. Sometimes other kids are better judges of characters than worried adults." *Jo, Winchester*

"I know I had friends that my parents didn't like when I started secondary school. I didn't realise they weren't good for me for another couple of years. But I had to learn that lesson for myself. You need to get into the wrong crowd, sometimes, to work out your own values in life. And parents can't do that for you." *Will, 17*

'I've fallen out with my friends'

It's awful when this happens. They come home from school distraught because they've fallen out with their best friend and there's nothing you can do about it. Or is there?

You have to play this one very carefully. Your instinct, as a caring parent, might be to jump in and make everything all right. You want to phone up this horrid child and tell them what a nasty little thing they've been. Then you want to tell their parents.

But if you do, you'll make it far worse. This child won't like being told off by another parent and you'll probably destroy any chance of reconciliation. Even worse, your child might well be teased by others who get to hear of the situation.

In our experience, the best remedy is to be there for your child. Comfort them and suggest they team up with someone else instead. They might tell you that everyone else has a best friend, which may well be true. So reassure them that, in time, someone will be a friend for them and that it really will get better.

This might not sound as though you're doing very much, but simply understanding will help your child feel better. Point out times when this has happened to their friends or siblings. Tell them about your own experiences. It always makes someone feel better when they realise they're not alone.

Psychologist and mother Gaynor Sbuttoni has some very sensible additional comments to make. "Acknowledge how horrible it is for them to fall out with their friends. As parents, we want to make it all right for them but they need to learn how to handle it. We can help by saying 'This must make you feel horrible, but what would you like to do about it?' If they say they don't know, say 'What do you think about this idea?' then you could suggest that they make friends with someone else. They might not like that idea but it could start them thinking about alternatives ."

"My 12 year old daughter wasn't invited on an outing which was being organised by a mother whom I knew well. Our daughters were great friends so naturally my child was really upset. She asked me not to say anything but I genuinely felt a mistake must have been made. So I rang the mother, pretending to talk about something else and then casually mentioned the outing. She immediately became very frosty and changed the subject. Unfortunately, her daughter then told mine that I'd inter-fered and the two of them haven't spoken since. I told my child that the other one wasn't worth getting upset about. But I'd never interfere again." Kim, mother of three, Middlesborough

When something sad happens to their friends

I've lost count of the number of times, over the years, that my children's 'best friend' has moved away. My own kids have, understandably, been heartbroken. But you can help them through it. Encourage them to keep up contact through phone calls and emails and My Space. Arrange regular visits, if possible, via their parents. And slowly wait until they make new friends at school – because they will. They may never be the same as the old friend but it will be a lesson that friends in life can come and go. It's also a lesson that even though a best friend is no longer round the corner, you can still keep him or her if you make the effort to maintain contact.

The serious illness or death of a friend is very difficult to help your children through. Sadly, we've had experience of this too. Hold and comfort your child. Explain how and why it happened as honestly as you can. Many children feel very vulnerable themselves when someone close to them dies or is ill. So explain that although this has happened to their friend, it's not likely to happen to them too.

Personally, I think it helps a child to be allowed to go to the funeral. It provides a closing chapter and it helps to let out grief. If your child becomes withdrawn – and who can blame them – you will need professional help. Ask your GP to recommend a counsellor or perhaps there's a family friend or older brother or sister who can help. Cruse runs a bereavement service for young children. **www.crusebereavementcare.org.uk**. See also the Bereavement Trust at **www.childbereavement.org.uk** Tel. 01494 446648.

Your child could also be helped by helping others. I have a friend whose teenage daughter was tragically killed in a car crash and she was greatly helped by her daughter's friends who took it in turns to visit her. Maybe your child could do the same if you feel they're up to it.

"Everyone in my daughter's class was very shocked when one of the girls developed cancer. Some of them were scared that because she got ill, they

could too. But the school was very understanding and brought in a counsellor who specialises in children's illnesses to talk to them. Sadly, the girl died but the counsellor came back for several more sessions to help them through. " **Maxine, London**

CHAPTER 9

How to beat the bully – and what to do if it's your child

Nowadays, schools claim to take bullying very seriously. But, in practice, it's not always easy to do something about it. If you think your child is being bullied, find a quiet time when you can talk to them about it. Find out what the bully is doing or saying and where.

You might feel it's not worth making a fuss about. Perhaps you can just advise your child to ignore it and walk off. But if it is serious, and by that we mean that your child is extremely upset, you should alert the school. Start off with the class teacher and/or year head but make sure that the subject is treated confidentially. Children hate it when their parents complain about other children because the bullies often make it worse by saying 'Your parents complained'. On the other hand, you can't let certain bullying pass without reporting it.

How to tell if your child is being bullied

Warning signs include:

- Reluctance, on your child's part, to go to school.

- Physical signs such as bruising.

- Missing personal possessions which your child has suddenly 'lost' like phone, iPod etc.

- Refusing to take the usual route to school.

What to do

- Talk to your child and gain their confidence.

- Talk to the teachers.

- Don't approach the parents directly. Even if you know them well, they might react in an unexpected way.

- Don't dismiss bullying as 'part of school life'.

- Log onto specialist websites such as **www.kidscape.org.uk**.

- Find out if the bully has upset other children and what their parents did about it. You could do this by quietly talking to other families.

- Find out what the school policy is on bullying. If you feel the school isn't treating this seriously, contact the governing board and local authority if it's a state school.

- Teach your child certain strategies to deter bullies. For example, if they walk tall and avoid eye contact with bullies, they might not be picked on so easily.

Advice from Kidscape for children on how to deal with bullies

You might like to show this to your kids as it's directed at them. Mind you, it's also worth trying it in the office if you have a bully of a boss.

- *Tell a friend what is happening.* Ask him or her to help you. It will be harder for the bully to pick on you if you have a friend with you for support.

- *Try to ignore the bullying or say 'No' really firmly, then turn and walk away.* Don't worry if people think you are running away. Remember, it is very hard for the bully to go on bullying someone who won't stand still to listen.

- Try not to show that you are upset or angry. Bullies love to get a reaction – it's 'fun'. If you can keep calm and hide your emotions, they might get bored and leave you alone. As one teenager said to us, 'they can't bully you if you don't care'.

- Don't fight back if you can help it. Most bullies are bigger or stronger than you. If you fight back you could make the situation worse, get hurt or be blamed for starting the trouble.

- It's not worth getting hurt to keep possessions or money. If you feel threatened, give the bullies what they want. Property can be replaced, you can't.

- Try to think up funny or clever replies in advance. Make a joke of it. Replies don't have to be wonderfully brilliant or clever but it helps to have an answer ready. Practise saying them in the mirror at home. Using prepared replies works best if the bully is not too threatening and just needs to be put off. The bully might just decide that you are too clever to pick on.

- Try to avoid being alone in the places where you know the bully is likely to pick on you. This might mean changing your route to school, avoiding parts of the playground, or only using common rooms or lavatories when other people are there. It's not fair that you have to do this, but it might put the bully off.

- Sometimes asking the bully to repeat what they said can put them off. Often bullies are not brave enough to repeat the remark exactly so they tone it down. If they repeat it, you will have made them do something they hadn't planned on and this gives you some control of the situation.

- Keep a diary of what is happening. Write down details of the incidents and your feelings. When you do decide to tell someone, a written record of the bullying makes it easier to prove what has been going on.

Use words as weapons against bullying

Says Heather Summers, neurolinguistic expert and mother: "Knowing what to say back to a bully can really help. Try these tips":

What a child can say to themselves

Before using words to deter bullies a child can be taught how to sit, stand and move so that they look more confident than they may feel. They can also practise speaking in a way that will prevent people from bothering or bullying them. And they can practise noticing what is happening around them so that they can avoid or prevent most trouble before it starts. In order to do this successfully it's good for a child who is being bullied to repeat phrases like:

'I am as good as anyone else. I deserve to be treated well by other people.'

'If they want to tease me, it's perfectly OK. They can do it all day long and it doesn't bother me in the least because I know that I am a worthwhile person.'

What a child can say out loud to bullies

This is reverse psychology and may seem odd, but is one of the most effective ways of dealing with it. If someone makes a nasty remark, simply say '...yeah, whatever.....' each time so that you show them that it isn't having the effect of upsetting you in the way they think.

- For example: 'If you want to call me names, that's OK'; or, 'If you enjoy making fun of me, you can do it all day long.' This will stop them very quickly. Just make sure to say it without any anger at all. And you must really mean it when you say it.

- For example, someone insults you or someone you care about. 'Your mother sleeps around.' Ask, 'Do you believe it?' If they say yes, then say, 'Well you can believe it if you want to. That's your choice.' Then walk away. Repeat this as often as you need to, but don't get into an argument by trying to defend your mother. This makes it worse.

- For example, someone asks you for your lunch money or something you own. Say 'I'd like to give you that but I can't.' Keep repeating this so that you don't get involved in a debate.

- For example, someone steals something from you. Say 'I would like my purse back, and I really don't want to get any-one in trouble.' If they don't get the message or return the purse, then you can report it to the appropriate adults. This is theft.

What not to say

Do nothing to make them stop:

- Do not tell them to stop.
- Do not call them names back.
- Do not hit them back.
- Do not get angry back.

This is what they are wanting. By not responding in the way they want they will eventually get bored and give up. Responding simply feeds a bully and encourages them to continue.

What if your child is the bully?

Yes, of course it's embarrassing. And yes of course you thought your child would never do anything like that. But it happens.

You might not know until school contacts you. Or you might find out through the parent grapevine. Either way, you need to sit down with your child and find out why he or she has behaved like that. Again, a non-aggressive attitude is much more likely to get a response than a 'How could you do this sort of thing?' approach.

Try getting to their emotional roots. Do they know how it feels to upset someone else? Do they realise that what they did is bullying? Verbal assaults are just as damaging, sometimes, as physical ones. Is it because they were bullied by someone else?

The website **www.directgov.co.uk** suggests that some bullies might be copying the behaviour of other people in the family. Perhaps they haven't learned better ways of mixing with their friends. Friends may be encouraging bullying or your child may be going through a difficult time and acting out aggressive feelings.

To stop your child bullying:

- Explain that what they are doing is unacceptable and making other children unhappy.

- Discourage other members of your family from using aggression or force to get what they want.

- Show your child how they can join in without bullying.

- See your child's teacher to talk about how you can work together to stop your child bullying.

- Check regularly with your child about how things are going at school.

- Give your child lots of praise when they are co-operative and kind to others.

Using the right words and phrases is very important. Neurolinguistic expert Heather Summers suggests asking your child the following questions:

- What's troubling you at the moment?

- When do you not feel good about yourself?

- What can I do to help make you feel better about yourself?

- What happens when you bully someone – how does it make you feel?

- Is there any other way you can get that good feeling without making someone else feel bad?

Heather also suggests the following exercise. "Let's say your child's name is Keith. Put a piece of paper with the name of the child being bullied on it on the floor. Let's say his name is Tom. Ask your child to stand on that piece of paper, and say 'I want you to imagine you are Tom. Imagine you are at school and that you are looking out through Tom's eyes. Now imagine that you (Tom) see Keith coming towards you. What do you feel?' (Wait for answers). ('Remember you are in Tom's shoes; you are Tom'). 'What happens now?' (Ask 'Tom' to describe what's happening and how he feels when he is being bullied by Keith.)

"'Now step out of Tom's shoes and be yourself again.' (Ask Keith to step off the piece of paper with Tom's name on it and to now face it). 'Now how do you feel when you look at Tom? How could you make Tom feel better about himself? What are you going to do differently from now on?'"

Take it from us...

"My daughter was hit in the face during a sleepover. She was asleep so she didn't know who did it although we have a good idea. The mother, who was holding the sleepover, was very embarrassed but she didn't know who it was either and none of the girls would own up. My daughter was so upset that she refused to go to school for a week. When she did, all the girls who'd been at the sleepover ignored her and said she'd got them into trouble. I told the teacher but she said there was nothing she could do as the incident had happened outside school. My daughter was miserable for the rest of the term but then I asked for her to be put in another class. She is now much happier." Mike, London

"My son kept getting abusive texts and then someone posted something nasty about him on a website. We were able to trace who had sent it and I went round to the parents. I pointed out that we could take legal action if they didn't put a stop to this. The messages stopped but my son was very upset for some time afterwards. I don't know if you can really stop bullying but you can be there for them if it happens." *Jan, St Albans*

"My son was beaten up by classmates after a school dance and he absolutely didn't want me to talk to school about it." *Name withheld*

THE EXPERTS SAY...

"Ask your child's school to consider a 'secret buddy' system where an older child can observe what is going on and report back to teachers." Margaret McGowan, ACE. ACE (the Advisory Centre for Education) has just published a booklet called 'Sorting It Out' £2. (See end for address).

Where to go for help

www.bullying.co.uk
www.kidpower.org
www.kidscape.org.uk
Parentline Plus 0808 800 2222

CHAPTER 10

'I don't feel well!'

It always happens when it's least convenient, doesn't it? And this is the one day you simply have to go into the office... But are they well enough to leave? Are they feeling ill because they're just tired? Are they making excuses because they don't like a lesson that day, or dislike school full stop?

Use your gut instinct

Take their temperature and feel their pulse. Do they look pale? Do they feel hot? Is there something going round at school?

If they are genuinely off colour, you're going to have to make alternative arrangements for someone to look after them. That might mean ringing your boss, or it could be finding someone to 'sit' with them. Even if you've never had this problem before at primary school, it's worth making emergency arrangements now in case it happens. Do you have a neighbour whom you could call on at the last minute?

If they are genuinely off-colour, don't be tempted to think they'll be all right once they get to school. I once had a really embarrassing incident when I sent my peaky son off only to get a call from the school office an hour later. "Your son told us that he didn't feel well when he got up," the school secretary said to me accusingly. I hung my head shamefacedly and failed to get elected onto to the PTA committee the following term.

If, on the other hand, you're pretty certain that your child is putting it on, you need to find out why. In one way, this is just as serious as an illness. You might not have time right now for an indepth emotional discussion on this, especially if you have to get to work. But later that evening, you need to sit down and find out what is going wrong. Are they being bullied? Pretending to be ill is a classic reaction to this. Are they worried about a test or exam that day? Are they happy generally?

If you're not sure whether they're ill or not, it might be worth keeping them at home that day just in case. But don't let them think they've 'got away with it'. Warn them that they're not allowed to play on the computer, iPod or whatever, and make it clear that if they feel better later on, you'll take them into school. If you're still uncertain, you could encourage them to get on with homework or coursework. That way, they'll know that staying at home isn't an easy option.

"And after you've done your homework you can tidy your room, change your sheets, mop the kitchen floor and put the rubbish out."

Are you being over fussy?

I know of one mother who keeps her kids at home at the mere sound of a sneeze. Some of us suspect she does so because she doesn't like being alone at home. It's easy to be paranoid about our children being ill, especially if we've had a bad experience before. If you're worried this applies to you, talk to your GP or another understanding parent. If we're too fussy, we might pass this onto our children and that won't be doing them any favours.

Catching up

One tricky thing about starting secondary school is that if your child misses a day or so of school, it's up to them to catch up the work. Now this is fine if you have a conscientious child. But some children will need nagging to check they have done this. It's also worth ringing school to find out what the protocol is on this. Should your child borrow another child's book to copy what they've missed? Or will the teacher organise this? Some teachers just expect kids to do this automatically but it isn't always something that occurs to a new child. And you can bet your bottom dollar that when it comes to exams or tests, your child will have missed something vital unless they've caught up.

By the way, this also applies if they've missed just one class for a music lesson, or an orthodontist appointment, or a visit to the doctor. If your child is still new, they might need prompting. Which lessons have they missed? How can they find out what happened? Was any homework set during those lessons which they need to be aware of?

You can see why kids need their own secretaries, can't you? They're called 'parents'…

When it's serious

If your child is off school for more than a week, you need to talk to someone at school to find out how they can catch up. If they're well enough, they might need extra lessons. If they're still poorly, are they well enough to have work set for them at home?

Local authorities have a duty to provide education for a child if they are unable to get into school for a substantial amount of time. Talk to school and your local education authority to see what can be done. It might be that the LEA sends a teacher round to your house. Also see the next chapter, *I don't want to go to school*.

Writing a note of absence

Most schools insist that parents write a note, explaining why their child was off school. This will also apply if your child has to leave school early or miss a lesson. Find out what the school rules are on this. I once 'earned' my son a detention by not doing it.

CHAPTER 11

I don't want to go to school

There's a big difference between a mild reluctance to go to school in the first week and refusing to go full stop. Or you might find your child has settled down quite happily but then goes off school in later years. So what should you do if they refuse to go?

According to the Royal College of Psychiatrists (RCP **www.rcpsych.ac.uk**), there are three reasons why children won't go to school; refusal, truancy and 'condoned absence', in other words parents who allow them to stay at home.

School refusal

"Your child may be too anxious to go to school,' warns the RCP. "Worrying about going to school can make them feel vaguely unwell with sickness, headaches, tummy aches, poor appetite and frequent visits to the loo. The symptoms are usually worse on weekday mornings and tend to disappear later in the day. This is sometimes called 'school phobia'.

"However, the problem does not always lie with school. A child may seem to be worried about going to school when actually they are fearful about leaving the safety of their home and parents. They can be rather clingy and lacking in confidence. Once they get involved in lessons and seeing their friends, they may find that they enjoy school."

What causes school refusal? The RCP points out that family

problems can be to blame. For example, a change in the family such as the birth of a brother or sister, a parent being ill or a death in the family.

So where do you find help? The RCP suggests talking to your child's teachers to see if they're aware of underlying problems. Most schools have an educational psychologist or welfare officer. It's also vital to eliminate any physical illness so see your GP. Talk things over with your GP, too, who might feel your child needs to be referred to the local child and adolescent mental health service. Try not to see this as a stigma. Your child needs help. Maybe your child might be able to confide in a family friend or older child.

Take it from us...

"My 13 year old daughter refused to go to school for three months after we moved from a different area and my marriage broke up. She just sat on the sofa and wouldn't talk to me. No one could get through to her. At first I panicked and begged her to be sensible. But then I found that it was far better to be calm and just accept what was happening. Then, one day, I suggested we went to look at another school and she agreed. Now it's as though it never happened. I think the trauma of my marriage breaking up and moving house had got to her. She just needed time to adjust." *Name withheld*

"When my daughter started refusing to go to school, her teacher organised a buddy for her – an older girl. She would arrive at our house in the morning to walk with her to school and to be there for her at break time. If your child's school doesn't have a buddy system, it's worth asking if they can start one." *Alison, High Wycombe*

Truancy

Not all kids who truant are bad. Most children go through a stage of trying it out, especially if they don't want to go to a school service such as Founder's Day, or they think they can bunk off early from sport.

Having said that, it's vital to nip it in the bud before it gets worse. If they haven't already got into trouble, point out that they could and might still do so. As with school refusal, see if a family friend or older sibling might be able to point out the stupidity of bunking school.

If you find it hard to talk to your child, ask to speak to the school's education welfare officer or educational psychologist. Also see your GP who might suggest you see the local child and adolescent mental health service.

The Department of Education also suggests that you try to prevent truancy by:

- Making sure your child understands how important it is to go to school on time.

- Taking an interest in your child's education by asking about work and so on.

- Listening to your child when they tell you about problems at school, and talking to the teacher or head about them if necessary.

"My 15 year old son started playing truant. Nothing we did could make him change until a friend, who's a nurse, sat down and talked to him. She focused on the positive instead of the negative. So she asked him which part of school he liked when he did attend. Through that, we found that he disliked certain subjects because he felt hopeless at them. We talked to school and they worked with us to increase his self-confidence." Rachel, Staines

"Ask your child if they're being bullied," advises Catherine Hanly, editor of Raising Kids. "They might not tell you at first, but this is often a reason for not wanting to go to school."

Parents who let their kids stay off school

Some parents will allow their children to stay at home because they know they won't go to school and feel it's better than wandering the streets. Some parents also become very anti-school, if they feel school is to blame for their child's behaviour. If you aren't happy with your child's school, there are other options such as finding somewhere different for them to go. But it goes without saying that missing school will seriously affect your child's education.

CHAPTER 12

Problems at school: telling school

If there are any problems at home, it's essential to tell school. If you don't and your child shows that they're upset through misbehaving or withdrawing from class activity, they might be told off without teachers realising the real cause.

Your child, on the other hand, might say they don't want the school to be told. That's because they are still a child and don't realise the importance of school and parents working together. You need to come clean and explain it's important for school to know but that you will ask them to keep it confidential.

What kind of problems?

School needs to know if you and your partner have split up. It also needs to know if there's been a close death in the family or if someone is seriously ill.

"One reason is that the class teacher might be doing a project on death or illness," says Moira, a teacher at a secondary school in Essex. "If he or she knows that there's a pupil in the class who has had direct and recent experience of this, they'll need to treat it with extra sensitivity. I once taught a girl whose parents didn't tell me that her grandmother had died. We did a project on Grandparents' Day and she ran out of the class, crying."

Not all teachers, sadly, take these problems as seriously as we would hope. I know someone who split up from her husband after a long marriage. Her daughter, understandably, began messing around at school and falling behind with work. Her class teacher, who was aware of the situation, called her mother in three months after the split and announced that she had given the child 'plenty of time' to get used to the new domestic situation and that she was running out of patience. The mother complained to the year head and pointed out that many children take years to get over a divorce. We can only hope that the message somehow got through to the (young and childless) teacher.

If you feel that school isn't taking your child's domestic problems seriously enough, see the year head and/or the head.

School counsellors

Most schools have a counsellor but they aren't always full time. If you are experiencing serious domestic problems, it might help your child to see one. Find out when the counsellor is available and how your child can make an appointment.

Not all children, however, want to see a counsellor and some will say they 'can't help'. Point out that it might benefit them to talk to someone who doesn't know them. Explain that it might make them feel better to get it off their chest. And assure them that it will be confidential and that no one else needs to know about it.

You might find that your child is happier talking to someone they do know, like a family friend, or an older brother or sister, or maybe a cousin. It's worth giving them the opportunity even if they say they don't need to talk.

Liz Holton at Hampshire County Council has some sensible guidelines on counselling in schools. She points out on their website that counselling can help with the following issues:

- When parents are going through divorce or separation, and the child is showing changes in behaviour or indications of distress.

- If there are known family relationship problems.

- When there is evidence of stress or a change in behaviour such as becoming withdrawn or disruptive.

- If there is a death of someone in the family, or a friend – even when the child seems to be coping.

- When there is knowledge or suspicion of some form of abuse or domestic violence.

- When there are difficulties with friendships, bullying or teasing.

- When a child, new to the school, is having difficulty settling or integrating.

- When a young person is angry, erratic or shows mood swings or depression.

- If there are drug, alcohol or eating problems or evidence of self-harm.

- When there is a sexual identity issue, racial discrimination or pressure to conform to cultural expectations.

- If there are health or disability issues.

- When you or their teachers regularly feel angry or exasperated with a student.

> **TOP TIP**
>
> Children can ask for counselling without their parents having to give written consent.

Who else could help?

The NSPCC works with certain schools to provide a counselling service. So if you feel your school isn't helping, contact the local branch.

Some parents also find their children are helped by alternative therapies such as hypnotherapy and acupuncture. Both can relieve stress in children as well as adults. To find a qualified practitioner in your area, contact The Hypnotherapy Association, 14 Crown Street, Chorley, Lancashire PR7 1DX, Tel 01257 262124, or email **theha@tiscali.co.uk**. For an acupuncturist, contact the British Acupuncture Council, 63 Jeddo Road, London, W12 9HQ, UK, Tel 020 8735 0400.

Depression

Sometimes, children at secondary school seem to get depressed for no obvious reason. It might be because they are hiding stress or because they can't do the work or have fallen out with friends and not told you. Signs of depression include:

- Not eating.
- Not sleeping.
- Irritability.
- Aggression.
- Not doing well at school.
- Staying in their rooms.
- Any unexplained change in behaviour.

If you feel your child might be depressed ask them, in a calm way, what is wrong. You could say 'I've noticed that you like staying in your room' or 'I can't help wondering why you're cross all the time. Would you like to tell me about it?'

If this doesn't work, try our previous advice of getting an older sibling, cousin or friend to see if they can find out what's wrong.

Depression can also be helped by improving your child's diet and encouraging them to exercise.

More help

- Check out Young Minds **www.youngminds.org.uk**, an excellent charity for helping adolescents and young people with problems, including mental difficulties.

- **www.nice.org.uk** The National Institute for Health and Clinical Excellence is an independent organisation responsible for providing national guidance on promoting good health, and the prevention and treatment of ill health
Tel 0870 155 5455

- **www.getconnected.org.uk** gives free, confidential help for young people.

Take it from us...

"My 16 year old son got very depressed when one of his cousins was killed in an accident. A friend of ours recommended hypnotherapy and I went with him. The hypnotherapist didn't put him out or send him into a trance as I'd expected. He spoke in a quiet melodic voice and my son later said it was like falling asleep without actually doing so. He talked to my son about how he felt and encouraged him to think of the happy memories he had with his cousin. We had three sessions and, afterwards, my son seemed more accepting of the situation." *Name withheld*

"My son got depressed when we moved areas. He didn't like his new school and one day, refused to get out of bed. He stayed there for a week. The GP came to talk to him and we promised to look at other schools. It took several months of counselling but now he's all right and happy at his new school." *Jill, Oxford*

CHAPTER 13

Fit enough for school?

One aspect of secondary school which shocks some parents – and disappoints certain kids – is that there might not be as much sport as there was at the previous school.

The government has an 'aspirational target' of providing two hours' worth of sport a week for children, and is hoping to raise this to four. Private schools usually offer much more.

If you feel your child's school doesn't provide enough sport, find out if there are after-school clubs – or suggest the school sets up specialist sports ones. Also talk to other parents and see if there are local clubs outside school that their kids go to. Your child might be keener to play hockey/take up athletics, if there's someone else in their class who wants to do the same.

Exercise is also fantastic for helping the brain to work better in class. So do as much as you can to get your child on the move.

Unfortunately, some kids go off sport during secondary school because they no longer think it's 'cool' or because they discover other kinds of 'sport' which they'd rather spend their free time on. I was really disappointed when one of my children decided to give up cricket because, as a county player, it took up too much of his weekend. But he became very enthusiastic about skateboarding instead – which also left him time to go to parties afterwards. I had to learn to accept this. After all, as my son told me in no uncertain terms, 'It's my life, mum, and not yours.'

Diet

One in four children are said to be overweight nowadays. That's partly due to exercise but diet is also crucial. When your child goes to secondary school, they'll have more freedom than before – and that includes the opportunity to buy snacks after school.

Similarly, they might be able to choose unhealthy lunches at school (providing Jamie Oliver hasn't taken over the kitchen).

So how can you encourage them to eat healthily? Try explaining why it's important. Food feeds the brain. If they eat the right food, they are less likely to get spots or put on weight. If you really want to get on their wavelength, tell them that eating the right food will improve their looks and increase their pulling power.

Here are some more ideas for getting your kids to eat a healthy diet.

- Point out food which is good for them like broccoli.

- Tempt their tastebuds at breakfast time by providing energy filled food which they like. I get up early to give my son a cooked bacon and egg breakfast.

- Suggest they take in a packed lunch.

- Try to get tea ready for them. Otherwise, they might start raiding the cupboards and eating snacks when you're still preparing the nutritious stuff.

- Consider having them tested for food allergies if you think they may have an intolerance or allergy. Ask your GP for help on this.

Also watch out for signs of eating disorders such as anorexia and bulimia. These might include:

- Skipping family meals.
- Pushing food round on the plate.
- Saying they've already eaten.
- Going to the loo after meals and being sick.
- Getting up in the night and binge eating.
- Counting calories excessively.
- Dry skin and puffy face (bulimia signs).
- Excessive use of fragrance sprays to hide the smell of vomit.
- Weighing themselves obsessively.

Helpful contacts

- **www.learntobehealthy.org** Gives advice on what it says.

- **http://www.allkids.co.uk/childrens-nutrition-and-healthy-eating.shtml** Also gives advice on nutrition and healthy eating.

- **http://www.raisingkids.co.uk/13_21/TEE_EAT.ASP** Raising Kids is an excellent website giving advice on bringing up children. This link has specific diet advice.

- **http://www.childrenfirst.nhs.uk/teens/health/healthy_eating/** Again, gives advice on diet.

- The Eating Disorders Association. Adult Helpline (over 18 years of age) 0845 634 1414 or Youthline (up to and including 18 years of age) 0845 634 7650. The EDA is a well known organisation for anyone with mental problems over food.

The book ***The Art of Hiding Vegetables*** *Sneaky ways to feed your children healthy food* by Karen Bali and Sally Child is full of ideas for giving children from toddlers to teens a healthy diet. White Ladder Press £7.99.

TOP TIP

Omega 3 and Omega 6 fish oil is said to boost brain power in both children and adults. Talk to your pharmacist and GP. If you're not sure your child is getting enough vitamins in their daily food intake, you might need to give them supplements.

"*My daughter started being fussy about her food when she was 15 and it wasn't 'cool' to have curves. I took her to the GP who referred her to a nutritionist. If anything, it made her worse because she became obsessed about how many calories she was eating. It got better when she went into the sixth form and some of the girls, who had criticised her for being 'tubby', left. But she's still very weight conscious. It just shows how influenced they can be by friends – and how parents can't always do anything about it.*" Sue, Liverpool

CHAPTER 14

School: enough to drive them to drink (and other things)

When your children start secondary school, they're going to come across a wider variety of children than they did before at primary school. This can be good but it can also lead to temptation of the kind you might not approve of.

No one likes to think their child will ever take drugs, drink too much or start smoking. But it happens. All you can do is try to minimise the chances and, if it happens, point out why it's not a good thing.

Give them the facts early on

Before they start secondary school, tell them why drugs, excessive drink and smoking are bad for their bodies. Download the facts from the net and put it in front of them. One useful website on drugs is **www.talktofrank.com**. This is designed to interest kids in the subject without talking down to them. It also has some really useful advice for parents. For example, at the time of going to press, the website had a report about the link between cannabis and mental health. You could print this out and either show it to your child or leave it in their bedroom. It also shows how drugs can affect the way you look. For example, kids can load a digital photo of themselves onto the site to see 'the ghoul-ish effects that drugs can have on your looks in real life!'

Alcohol is becoming a really big problem with teenagers, which can start when they get to secondary school (and sometimes ear-lier). The problem with this is that your teenagers probably see you enjoying a glass of wine or gin and tonic. So what's wrong with them doing the same?

We have to point out that there's a difference between a couple of glasses and binge drinking. And of course, if your kids are like mine, they'll dismiss us as fussy and boring. So try giving them the facts. Leave out newspaper reports with statistics.

The charity Parentline Plus (**www.parentlineplus.org.uk**) offers the fol-lowing advice:

- Talk openly about what you see as the potential dangers – from health to safety – in a practical way so they don't tune out.

- Get the timing right. Try to find a relaxed time when you can both chat, such as when you are giving them a lift, rather than when they are halfway out of the door or with their mates.

- Remember your own behaviour will influence them. Be hon-est about the reasons why you or people in general like drink-ing, as well as the negatives of alcohol.

- Talk about how they may feel or what they may do under pres-sure – whether it is deciding what they do if they are offered a drink, or if a friend offers them a lift home after drinking.

- Research shows that unprotected and early sex is often linked to alcohol. Take time to talk about how alcohol can influence people's judgement and help them to think through how it might feel to regret something the next day.

- Make them aware of drinks being spiked and not putting themselves in vulnerable situations. Get them and their friends to look out for each other. Explore how alcohol affects people in different ways, and how it can make some people aggressive and up for a fight. Talk through ways of keeping safe and walking away from trouble.

- Ensure your teens know that no matter how angry you may be with them you are there for them, so they will call you if someone gets hurt or they are worried about something.

- Gen up on the facts. You may want to talk about different drinks and their alcoholic strength – for example alcopops can taste just like fizzy drink, and without realising it the alcohol can have a huge affect.

- Try not to take it personally or feel downhearted if they don't take heed of your advice. Sometimes teens have to make their own mistakes to realise what you have said is true.

Alcohol facts

Youngsters aged 11-15 are drinking twice as much as they used to in the early 90s, with more than one in five now saying they drink at least once a week.

That's the warning issued at the start of National Parents' Week by Alcohol Concern, who are calling for improved education about the effects of alcohol and greater guidance for children from their parents.

In a new report revealing the latest available research on teenagers' drinking, Alcohol Concern says that the average weekly amount drunk by all 11-15 year olds was 1.6 alcohol units by the end of the 90s, compared with 0.8 units in 1990. Another startling statistic shows that those who were drinking were consuming on average almost 10 units a week by 1998, compared with 5.3 units in 1990.

There has also been a steady increase in the frequency of 11-15 year olds' drinking sessions, with the number saying they drink at least once a week rising to 21% by 1999, compared with 20% in 1996 and 17% in 1994.

"I got really worried when I smelt alcohol on my 15 year old son's breath but he assured me he'd just had a couple of beers at a school friend's party. I told him why it was important not to drink too much and we agreed to set a 'two drinks max' rule. Now when he goes to a party, he asks me to buy him six cans of lager and I agree. I believe it's better for him to be open with me about drink rather than him trying to get someone else to buy it for him. I know not everyone will agree with this but this way, he trusts me and I trust him." Name withheld

Get school involved

Ask your child's head of year about school's policy on giving talks about drugs and drink etc. When do they start giving these talks? Do they have teenagers to talk about it as well as adults? School might be interested in a scheme run by the Fairbridge charity in Middlesborough which uses special dolls to show children the effects of drugs and alcohol. Teenagers have to look after these dolls for two nights while they go through the shaking 'withdrawal' stage.

If drugs or alcohol are taken on the school's premises, it's school's responsibility to sort it out. Many schools have a zero tolerance policy. In other words, they expel pupils who drink or take drugs while at school. Maybe you ought to tell your child that.

THE EXPERTS SAY...

"It's really important to explain to teenagers that they could get a criminal record for misbehaving," warns Catherine Hanly, editor of *Raising Kids*. "Taking drugs is bad enough, but if they're caught supplying friends with drugs, it's very bad news. Teenagers don't always realise that if this goes on permanent record, they may not be able to go to America or college. If they know this, they might be less likely to do it."

So you've found cigarettes in your teenager's pocket...

When kids start secondary school, they are often influenced by other kids who smoke. They might do the same to look cool, because they want to fit in, or because they feel under stress. But what should you do? The charity Raising Kids (**www.raisingkids.co.uk**) has the following advice:

- *Talk*. Don't describe the terrible things that will happen to your child at 50. Thirty seems ancient to them and 50 plus is really out of the frame. Don't lecture or nag, however strongly you feel. Try to talk to them calmly and use arguments they might just respond to. Concentrate on immediate rewards – money saved for other (nicer) treats, sparkling teeth and fresh smelling clothes. Make the point that if they get hooked now, they'll definitely want to give up in five years. They ought to recognise the truth in this. The longer they smoke, the more difficult quitting will be. Some politically conscious teens are susceptible to arguments about the profits that big business reaps from weak willed teenagers.

- *Bribe*. Some parents find bribery works. A friend promised her son a large sum of money on his 18th birthday on the assumption that if he could last until then, he was unlikely to start later. Not a cast iron guarantee since many students start to smoke at university, but generally, the later they start the less likely they are to continue.

- *Count pennies.* Work out what it costs them to smoke every week and do a deal with them to break the habit in a month. For the first week, each day they put the money they save into a pot and you match the amount. In the second week, you give double the amount they save. In week three, three times and in week four, four times the amount saved. At the end of four weeks they will have amassed a tidy sum and broken the smoking habit. If they smoke in the four weeks, they forfeit the lot and you pocket it. This approach only works if they have a commitment to give up and saving money is the right incentive for them.

Smoking facts

A team from the University of Leeds looked at the smoking habits of teenagers over six years. The study confirmed that teenage girls are twice as likely as boys to take up the habit. Anti-smoking campaigners said population-wide measures were need-ed to cut teenage smoking rates.

This latest study involved 1,134 teenagers aged 15 to 16, and found that:

- At age 11 to 12, just 2% of boys and 2% of girls had been reg-ular smokers.

- However, by the time they were 13 to 14, 16% of girls and 8% of boys were regular smokers.

- And by age 15 to 16, 31% of girls and 16% of boys were smok-ing regularly.

The researchers used questionnaires, breath and saliva tests to assess the teenagers' smoking habits. The research was funded by the Economic and Social Research Council.

The good news, however, is that apparently some teenagers have stopped smoking because they can't afford to smoke and pay for their mobiles.

Where to get more help

- **www.alcoholandyou.org** Fact site aimed at teens about alcohol.

- **http://uk.dir.yahoo.com/Health/Teen_Health/Teen_Smoking/** Teen site on dangers of smoking.

- **www.ash.org.uk** Organisation giving help on giving up.

- **www.givingupsmoking.co.uk**. Includes a great A-Z index for teenagers on how to give up smoking.

CHAPTER 15

Schools and discipline

They might not be able to cane kids any more, but you need to be aware of the discipline procedures that school can take. Before your child starts school, find out what its policy is. For example, does school give detentions to pupils who don't behave? What might they give detentions for? How many pupils were expelled in the last year? Why? How many were given temporary suspensions? Why?

This might sound rather alarming but it's better to be forewarned than be taken by surprise. And if you've got the kind of child who answers back or doesn't always respect authority, it might not be a bad idea to warn him too.

Schools are meant to review their behaviour policies once a year and publicise them to parents, staff and pupils. The policy should set standards of behaviour and include a code of conduct for pupils.

Detentions

Your school has the legal right to give your child a detention either after school, during lunchtime, on a Saturday or a school holiday. If your child doesn't attend, they can be punished more severely (double detention, suspension and the like). Legally, you're entitled to 24 hours' written notice of a detention so you can make arrangements for transport or childcare. The notice should tell you why the detention was given and you usually have to sign it to prove receipt, rather like a parcel (although you may well feel like handing your child back to the office from which it came).

Some schools give detentions quite readily during the first two years of secondary school. "It's our way of keeping children in line," explained a teacher who didn't want to be named. "We do get some parents ringing us because their children have never had detentions before and are now upset. But we have to nip any potential trouble in the bud."

Your immediate response might be to accuse school of being unfair. Of course your son wasn't rude to the biology teacher. Or was he?

"Some children play the fool when they start secondary school because they feel vulnerable and out of their depth," explained the same teacher. "They feel good when they make other kids in their class laugh so they might mess around. And then they'll get detentions."

So if your child is suddenly getting told off even though he was well behaved at primary school, it's worth talking to him about why he's doing it. Explain that he doesn't have to mess around to earn friends – and that if he does, those kind of friends aren't the type worth having.

School rules

Make sure you know what the school rules are – and that your child does, too. Your child's school is bound to have a policy on things like:

- Earrings
- Tattoos
- Nail varnish

- Make up
- Smoking
- Skipping school
- Being rude
- Not handing in homework

Some schools make children write out the school rules as part of their detention. One of my offspring (I won't identify the culprit) knows his off by heart.

Temporary exclusion

This is for children who get into serious trouble. It means the child is excluded from school for a limited period of time. It cannot be for longer than a total of 45 days in a school year. If your child is excluded for more than a day, school has to give him work that is marked. The school is meant to call you on the day an exclusion is given and provide a letter explaining the length of time, the reasons and who to contact. Children can be excluded only if they have seriously broken school rules or if their presence at school would harm other children or disrupt learning.

Permanent exclusion

So the worst has happened and school has asked you to withdraw your child from school. What rights do you have?

If it's a private school, you might have very little comeback. You could appeal to the governors but if a major decision like this has already been made, it will probably already have the governors' approval. If you feel there were extenuating circumstances and that school has overreacted, you should say so in writing.

If it's a state school, you should start off by requesting an interview with the head and the governing body. Bring your child with you so they can answer any accusations. If you feel your child is being expelled unfairly, contact the local education authority, which will organise for you to appeal to an independent appeal panel. The LEA has a statutory duty to provide education for your child, even if a school has expelled them. However, this might be at home or at a special centre.

Some schools will temporarily suspend a pupil as a severe warning. If this happens, it is usually for a short period of time ranging from one day to a week or more. Pupils are set work at home. The punishment is intended to be a shock to the system – including yours.

Before accepting expulsion, contact ACE, the Advisory Centre for Education. It has experts who specifically advise on exclusion:

- General advice line: 020 7704 3397
- Exclusion information line: 020 7704 9822
- Exclusion advice line: 020 7704 3398

Take it from us...

"Our son was expelled for taking cannabis when he was 16. We had problems finding a state school which was happy to take him but, in the end, we discovered an understanding head. I can't say that the shock stopped him taking drugs but it did make him realise that there are certain boundaries he shouldn't cross. That made more of an impact than us telling him the same thing over the years. Now he's at university and we're still communicating. I actually think that's the most important thing because I know of kids who were expelled for the same reason and consequently thrown out of the house by their parents. In my view, that's a real tragedy." *Richard, London*

"Our 15 year old daughter was suspended for continually fail-
ing to hand in homework and for being rude to the teacher.
She had to stay at home for a week with homework set by
school. This was very inconvenient as I had to take a week off
work to keep an eye on her. I was terrified that if I didn't, she
might do something else that was wrong. I don't think the suspension did any good. In fact, it made it worse. She was very
resentful of school and I felt they should have sorted out her
problems in a more understanding way. She moved to a different school at 16 and we are very pleased with its attitude.
Our daughter no longer rebels because she isn't made to feel
like a troublemaker." *Margaret, Newcastle upon Tyne*

CHAPTER 16

When school isn't right for your child

Just as all children are different, so are all schools. And although your child's school might have seemed the best match for them when they started, the situation might change as they get older. So what should you do?

Don't make any hasty decisions

Children who go to lots of different schools often feel rootless and take time to settle. The effects can continue into adult life. So if your child says they dislike school, or you don't feel the teachers are doing their best for them, monitor the situation for a few months before jumping in at the deep end and hauling them out.

Talk to school about your concerns in a non-threatening manner. Involve your child in these meetings. They might be able to make points you can't and, at that age, they deserve to have a voice.

What are the options?

Consider these carefully. What other schools could they go to? How do you know they'd be any happier there? Of course you don't. But at least you've had some experience of secondary school life, so this time round you'll be better prepared when asking questions.

Visit alternative schools with your child and soak up the atmosphere. Don't volunteer information on why you're thinking of changing schools in case this clouds their view of you. And don't criticise the school your child is at. Schools tend to stick together when this happens.

If you can afford it, consider whether a private school might suit your child better. Make a list of the pros and cons. It might have a wider curriculum but can you cope with the cost? How many new boys or girls would be joining at the same time? If there aren't many, would your child feel different?

You might also want to consider boarding. Whatever your own views, some children really enjoy being with other children for an extended period of time. Look into the possibility of a scholarship or financial help if your budget is limited. Contact the Independent Schools Council **www.isc.co.uk**. Also ask yourself how you would cope if your child boarded. You won't be there to check they've done their homework or if they're feeling poorly. It will also affect the family dynamics at home when there is one child less.

Take it from us

"We have one daughter and three sons. The boys are always arguing and it's a very noisy house. Our daughter found this hard to cope with and she also felt 'over-brothered'. So we applied for a scholarship at an all girls boarding school. She loved it." *Suzanne, Northampton*

"My son boarded but I found it very difficult not having the daily contact with him. He always sounded quiet at the other end of the phone and I felt we were growing apart. After two years, we withdrew him and he went to a local school. I feel we're much more of a family now." *Name withheld*

Moving areas

Of course, your child might need to change schools because you're moving house. If you don't know the schools in your new area, get a list from the local education authority. Ring each school and ask to be put in touch with the Parents Teachers Association. Talk to some of the mothers about the schools and ask them to be frank. One good question is 'What are the school's strengths and what are its weaknesses?'

Education outside school

Legally, you are perfectly entitled to educate your children at home providing the education reaches a certain standard. The local education authority might want to see proof of this with home visits. You might also have to provide evidence your child is being properly educated, by writing a report and providing samples of your child's work. Although it's not legally imperative, it's a good idea to inform the local authority that you are educating your child at home. If you are withdrawing your child from school to home educate them, you have to tell them in writing. If the local authority believes that your child is not receiving a suitable education, it can serve a school attendance order which means you have to send your child to school.

Personally, I take my hat off to any parent who is happy to have their kids at home 24 hours a day, every day. But then again, all the home educated kids I've ever come across have been charming, articulate and highly intelligent. The fact that their parents looked exhausted had nothing to do with this, I'm sure... Seriously, if this might be an option for you, contact organisations like Education Otherwise and the Home Education Advisory Service, known as HEAS.

Both have introductory booklets and packs, explaining how you can get started. For example, you might feel qualified to teach your children yourself or you might hire a tutor. Many families get together to reduce the cost of this. There are also several home correspondence courses.

Legally, there is no obligation to take any exams or follow the National Curriculum. However, as a parent, you have to make sure your child receives full time education that's suitable to their age, ability and aptitude. You don't need to be a qualified teacher to educate your child at home. Nor do you have to have a fixed timetable or give formal lessons or holidays.

"OK I'll teach you French, maths and history if you'll teach me how to set the timer on the video and how to use spreadsheets."

Parents who support home education are often at great pains to point out that their children do not suffer from a lack of friends as they get together with other children who are also being schooled at home.

You can find out more from:

www.heas.org.uk
www.education-otherwise.com

Take it from us

"Our son's school seemed right for him for the first four years, but then we felt it wasn't stretching him enough so we moved him. Some schools are good for certain children at different ages." *Kim, London*

"I only started thinking about home education when our daughter was bullied so badly we couldn't send her back. We've joined a local group of home educators and our daughter is a different child. When she's older she might go to a sixth form college but we're leaving the option open to her." *Tony, Manchester*

"I liked my school but my parents said the teaching wasn't stretching me enough. So they moved me. I don't like the school they sent me to and now they say they wish they'd kept me at the first. When I'm a parent, I'm going to listen to what my kids want." *Stephanie, 13, London*

CHAPTER 17

What if your child has special needs?

The phrase 'special educational needs', otherwise known as SEN, means children with learning difficulties or disabilities that make it harder for them 'to learn or access education' than most children of the same age. For example, they might need help with:

- Reading
- Writing
- Number work
- Understanding information
- Making friends
- Behaving properly in school
- Organising themselves
- Any physical or emotional problem

The above information comes from **www.direct.gov.uk**. So if you have any complaints, please talk to them and not us.

Statements

Many children with special needs are 'statemented'. This means they are assessed in terms of what they can and can't do as well as how they should be helped. If your child has such a statement, you have a right to say whether you want them to go a mainstream or special school. Statements can also be reviewed if your child's needs change, extra help is needed, or your child moves to a different school.

Special schools usually take children with particular types of special needs. For example if your child has severe cerebral palsy. Many mainstream schools have facilities for physically disabled pupils or special teaching for children with dyslexia or hearing problems and so on. Legally, mainstream schools are not allowed to discriminate against disabled pupils. For example, they have to promote the inclusion of disabled pupils in admission arrangements. They also have to have an accessibility plan showing how they intend to improve accessibility for disabled pupils if necessary.

Some parents argue that their children with special needs do better in mainstream schools. This is often because they are pushed up and encouraged by the example of other children who don't have the same special needs that they do. However, some people argue that special needs children are held back at mainstream schools because they can't do things that other children can.

When choosing a school for your special needs child, talk to as many people as you can, including charities that specialise in your child's problem. Ask schools on your shortlist to tell you what their policy is on SEN.

"The school should try to include you in any discussions and consider your views in making decisions about your child," says a spokesman for Teachernet, which forms part of the Department for Education and Skills. "They should also try to get the views of your child wherever possible. The school may decide that your child needs extra or different help, which may be a different way of teaching certain things, some help from an adult, or use of particular equipment like a computer."

They're not making enough progress

"If your child doesn't seem to be making enough progress, the class teacher or the school's SEN Co-ordinator (known as the SENCO) should talk to you about getting advice from other people outside the school," says a spokesman for Teachernet (**www.teachernet.gov.uk**). "This might be from a specialist teacher, for example, or an educational psychologist, or a speech and language therapist, or another health professional. This kind of help is called Early Years Action Plus in early education settings, or School Action Plus in schools.

"In some cases, help provided by the school at School Action or School Action Plus may not be enough to ensure that your child makes progress. In this situation the school, having discussed the matter with you, can ask the local education authority (LEA) which is responsible for the school to carry out a Statutory Assessment of his or her special educational needs, taking account of specialist advice and your views as well. If the LEA decides after the assessment that your child needs more special help (and only around 3% of children nationally require this), it must write a Statement of Special Educational Needs, which is usually called a 'statement'. It describes the child's needs and all the special help he or she requires. The school can usually provide this help with the LEA's support. The statement is reviewed annually, and you will be invited to take part in review meetings."

Supposing your child isn't getting the help they were promised in their statement?

"First check with the school to see why," says a spokesman for the Department of Education. "Is it a short term problem due to a staff absence/equipment broken down? If you are not satisfied with the reasons but feel the support set out is correct, you should contact the Special Educational Needs and Disability Division, Area 4D, Caxton House, 6-12 Tothill Street, London SW1H 9NA or email sen.queries@dfes.gsi.gov.uk."

If you do not think the provision set out is meeting your child's needs you can request a reassessment of your child's SEN. If this is declined or you disagree with a proposed amended statement you can appeal to the SEN & Disability Tribunal.

Special needs facts

These might look a bit stodgy but they could be useful if you are campaigning for a different kind of education for your child. This information comes from BBC NEWS UK SYSTEMS.

- All local education authorities and state schools in England have to follow a government code of practice on how to identify, assess and monitor pupils with special needs.

- An estimated one in five children has some form of special educational need, ranging from mild dyslexia to behavioural problems to complex medical conditions.

- In most cases this is dealt with in schools through an individual action plan. But some children need more support than their school can provide.

- For these children, the local authority draws up a statement of special educational needs, which in most cases provides extra help of some kind in the school.

- Just over 3% of children in England and Wales have a statement.

- Provision varies between authorities. Parents have a right to appeal to a Special Educational Needs Tribunal if they disagree with the statement.

- The Special Educational Needs and Disability Act 2001, which applies to England and Wales and in part in Scotland, reinforces the right of children with physical or behavioural problems to be taught in mainstream classes. It was backed by the promise of money to improve access in schools and colleges.

- The new law makes it illegal to treat disabled pupils 'less favourably' than other pupils and requires schools to make 'reasonable adjustments' so that disabled pupils are not put at a 'substantial disadvantage'.

- The government has made it clear that it wishes to see more special needs children entering mainstream schools. As a result, special schools for children with moderate difficulties are being closed in many areas.

- In 2000, 60% of pupils with statements were in maintained mainstream schools, 35% were in special schools and 5% were in independent schools.

- There are about 2,000 special schools (both day and boarding) for pupils with special educational needs. Some of these are run by voluntary organisations and some are in hospitals.

- The average pupil-teacher ratio in special schools is 6.5:1 compared to 18.6:1 in mainstream state schools and 9.9:1 in independent schools.

- Some independent schools provide education wholly or mainly for children with special educational needs, and are required to meet similar standards to those for maintained special schools. It is intended that pupils should have access to as much of the national curriculum as possible.

School transport

If your child has special needs, contact your LEA about transport to school. LEAs can make decisions according to the case. You might also be able to get financial help if you take your child to school yourself. Again, contact your LEA.

> *"Our 12 year old son has Downs Syndrome. He is bright but slightly dyslexic. We wanted to send him to an independent school which selects pupils through a test. He sailed through the tests and has now thoroughly integrated with the pupils and is very happy. But some of our friends continue to express surprise that he isn't at a 'special school'. If you have a special needs child, he or she is perfectly entitled to mainstream schooling providing it suits them."* **Angela, Southampton**

CHAPTER 18

Dealing with difficult teachers – without destroying your child's school career

There aren't any easy answers here. Basically, it's difficult to win with difficult teachers because they know they are right. Sometimes it's not worth trying because you can set them against your child. We've come across teachers who immediately take it out on children by being sarcastic or unfair to them in class, because their parents have complained. It shouldn't happen but it does because – and your child might disagree with this – teachers are human.

There are, however, certain tactics which are worth following. The first rule is to beware of going in with all guns firing.

"If you're not happy with a teacher, I'd suggest talking to that teacher first of all," says Sue Foreman of the National Association of Schoolmasters Union of Women Teachers (NASUWT). "Start off by saying 'I've come here to find a resolution to this problem and I'd like to work together with you.'"

If you still don't get anywhere, see the year head and then the head. Every school should have a set complaints procedure. If it's a state school, this should be agreed with the union, human resources and the local authority.

It's also worth talking confidentially to other parents. Some teachers turn out to have dubious past behaviour but school has hushed this up. We spoke to one mother, who asked not to be identified, whose son had been hit on the knuckles with a ruler by a teacher who had done the same with other pupils who had stepped out of line. The mother complained to the head but the teacher was merely reprimanded. It was only when she spoke to other parents that she found out the teacher had done this before.

On the other hand, you have to be careful not to get a reputation for stirring discontent amongst other parents. So tread carefully. It all goes to show that apart from being a nanny, a chauffeur and the owner of a bottomless purse, a parent also needs to be a good spy.

Sometimes, you just have to accept that a difficult teacher is a lesson in life. Bob Carstairs, assistant general secretary of the Association of School and College Leaders (ASCL) suggests pointing out to your child that a difficult teacher is 'an irritant in a minor part of your life'. In other words, he/she won't be there for ever. "There's no point in saying you will make it all right because that won't happen. In many ways, it's a good lesson for them because it shows they won't be able to get on with everyone in life."

On the other hand, if you feel a teacher is not doing their job properly or simply can't get their subject across, you're perfectly entitled to complain.

TOP TIP

"One in four maths lessons in English secondary schools is taught by a teacher who has never been trained in the subject." *From a report in* The Independent

Take it from us

"I had to speak 'in confidence' to a school about a problem with my child. The teacher then spoke to my child and it was obvious I had spoken to the school. My son was furious and I felt betrayed by the teacher." *Name withheld*

"Don't allow a difficult teacher to colour your perception of school. If you 'downtalk' it or criticise it, you'll encourage your child to dislike it too. So try and be positive." *Anne, Poole*

"One of our daughters was bullied by a teacher on a school trip. The teacher had many problems of her own and after complaints from many of us, went on long term sick leave. Our other daughter was bullied and undermined by a teacher who refused to believe in her abilities. We talked it through with the teacher who was not interested. Our daughter didn't want us to take it further. She did very well at GCSE but the teacher remained uninterested."
Sandra, Brighton

"Our son was in a small year group because he had dyslexia but I feel some staff could have been more tolerant and patient by showing him how to do things several times if necessary. I also think they should have supported the right behaviour rather than constantly drawing attention to the wrong, which only resulted in more wrong behaviour. However, I tried to do the 'repair' work at home because I think teachers get annoyed if you complain."
Name withheld

"One of our sons was bullied by a teacher who hit him without reason. I had already decided to move my son anyway so I didn't complain. I knew other parents had had solicitors in to talk to the teacher in the past but I decided not to follow suit as our daughter was still there. Sometimes you have to make decisions like that to protect your children. This teacher was very powerful and would have made life impossible for our daughter if we'd made a stand." *Name withheld*

"Some teachers can be very sarcastic and use it as a put-down to control pupils. Others try to be too matey and then wonder why they can't keep control." *Name withheld*

THE EXPERTS SAY...

"Don't act in haste," advises Raising Kids. "It's easy to race round to school and get upset. Calm down and work out what you're going to say in a non-aggressive way. You'll get much further that way."

"Help your child to understand that teachers are under pressure too," says Professor Cary Cooper. "They don't always have the time."

"Use parents' evening to find out what the problem is between the teacher and your child," recommends Margaret McGowan, parent and advisor for ACE. "Officially, teachers don't bully but it can happen. Say something like 'My daughter enjoys your classes but there seem to be some difficulties. Can you tell me more about that.' Then use whatever information you get to try and resolve the situation. For example, if your child is always answering back, you can discuss this with them and try to work out what they could do instead. If you're still unhappy about a teacher, try and get some mediation with another teacher or even ask if your child can be moved. On the other hand, children also need to learn that not everyone is going to like them in life. There are, however, ways of dealing with this such as keeping a low profile."

"Try and see it from the teacher's point of view," advises Catherine Hanly, editor of *Raising Kids.* "It might help you and your child to find an answer."

CHAPTER 19

What exactly do they do all day? Understanding the National Curriculum

From the ages of 11 to 16 your child will move through Key Stages 3 and 4. These stages cover all of their compulsory secondary education, including their subject and GCSE choices in Year 9.

Key Stage 3 and the National Curriculum

Children attending a state school from ages 11 to 14 (Years 7 to 9), study at Key Stage 3 of the National Curriculum.

Key Stage 3 compulsory National Curriculum subjects are:

- English
- Maths
- Science
- Design and technology
- Information and Communication Technology (ICT)
- History
- Geography
- Modern foreign languages
- Art and design
- Music
- Citizenship

- Physical education

Your child will also receive:

- Careers education
- Religious education
- Sex education

However, schools are given guidance only on how these subjects should be taught.

Depending on the school, your child may also receive provision in:

- Personal, social and health education (PSHE)

Children generally choose which GCSEs they're going to do – known as GCSE options – at the end of Year 9. Schools generally have their own policies on how many exams children take and you should be given lots of opportunities to discuss this with the teachers.

Be realistic. If your child's school doesn't think they're up to doing a certain subject, listen to their views and talk it over with your child. Many subjects have a higher and intermediate level. Then again, one of my children was very upset when he was told he should do an intermediate level in science. We argued that he should do the higher level and he got an A grade. So follow your parental instinct too.

Key Stage 4

Pupils in Years 10 and 11 are usually between the ages of 14 and 16 years old. They are now in Key Stage 4 and, at the end of this stage, will normally sit national examinations, usually GCSEs. Your child will also be able to choose from a growing range of vocational qualifications.

In Key Stage 4, your child will study a mix of compulsory and optional subjects. The subjects they will have to do are:

- English

- Maths

- Science

- Information and Communication Technology (ICT)

- Physical education

- Citizenship

- Religious education, careers education, work related learning and sex education (these are compulsory, but not part of the National Curriculum)

Your child will also be able to study one subject from each of the four 'entitlement' areas:

- The arts
- Design and technology
- Humanities
- Modern foreign languages

Wider choice

Over the next 10 years, 14 to 19 year olds will be offered greater choice in the courses, subjects and qualifications they take, making it easier to gain the basic skills needed for life and work. New Specialised Diplomas will be introduced alongside GCSEs and A levels.

New Specialised Diplomas

Under the new system, students will be able to follow a course in one of 14 Specialised Diplomas, which means they can focus sooner on the subjects that matter to them. Shaped by employers and universities, the Diplomas will offer more opportunities for practical learning.

Five of the specialised Diplomas will be introduced from 2008. These will cover:

- ICT (Information Communication Technology)
- Engineering
- Health and social care
- Creative and media industries
- Construction and the built environment

Five more Diplomas will be introduced from 2009:

- Land based and environmental
- Manufacturing
- Hair and beauty
- Business administration and finance
- Hospitality and catering

The final four Diplomas, in public services, sport and leisure, retail, and travel and tourism will be introduced from September 2010. From September 2013, wherever young people are in the country, they will have the choice between all the Specialised Diplomas, alongside the National Curriculum.

Changes to GCSEs and A levels

Why is it that every government seems to feel compelled to make changes every few years? As long suffering parents, pupils and teachers know to their cost, change isn't always for the best.

Under this lot of new changes, GCSE English, maths and ICT will include 'functional' skills that young people will find useful for their adult life and the world of work. A new General Diploma, currently being developed, will be awarded to those kids who achieve the equivalent of five GCSEs at grade A*-C including English and maths.

There will also be a '14 to 16 Re-engagement Programme' which will help young people to develop basic skills such as literacy and numeracy, and personal and social skills such as teamwork.

The number and type of A levels you can take is usually determined by the GCSE grades. Many schools won't allow a child to do an A level in a subject unless they get a C grade or higher. According to your child's academic capabilities, they will either do three or four AS levels, and then three A levels. But some children drop an AS level or only take three in the first place. The final A level grades are determined by the number of points gained in each exam. Yes, we've got a headache too.

Some schools will also ask pupils to leave if they don't get adequate grades at AS level. So find out what the school policy is. Or choose a school that doesn't throw them out halfway through.

International Baccalaureate

An increasing number of English schools, especially in the private sector, are replacing A levels with the International Baccalaureate. They are doing so because it offers a wider range of subjects and is recognised in many European countries as a good indication of academic performance.

Sets

By the time they get to Year 9, many pupils are put into sets according to their capabilities. Try not to get too uptight about this. So your child is in the bottom group of French? Then they're probably feeling pretty awful anyway. Instead of saying 'How did that happen?', consider how you could help them. Can you afford extra coaching? Can you help them yourself?

"I was upset when my son was put in the bottom division for maths. But he actually thrived in a smaller group which had a fantastic teacher. And he got better grades in his GCSE than some of his friends in higher groups." **Karen, Reigate**

TOP TIP

Around half of all students who take their GCSEs get fewer than five at grade C or above. (Information from **www.direct.gov.uk**).

Gifted and talented kids

If you're lucky (?) enough to have one of these, you might be interested to know that the government has introduced a 'gifted and talented' programme for children. According to its blurb, 'gifted' learners have abilities in one or more academic subjects like maths and English. Talented learners have particular abilities in sport, music, design or creative and performing arts.

If you think your child falls into either of these categories, talk to his or her teacher or head. Some schools and local authorities also have a gifted and talented co-ordinator.

Schools have a legal responsibility to meet the educational needs of all their pupils, including those who are gifted and talented. If you don't feel this is happening, contact the National Association for Gifted Children (NAGC). It runs an independent parent support network to help parents resolve disputes with schools and local authorities.

CHAPTER 20

How to help your teenager to learn

Sadly, nagging doesn't usually work. Trust us on this one. We've tried – again and again. The good news is that you can help them learn through providing a comfortable warm home environment with a quiet spot for working. Plenty of food at regular intervals helps too.

Most schools nowadays provide lessons in how to memorise facts, such as teaching them to mindmap (see next chapter on exams). But if they don't, you could help them do this. Check out sites like **www.nap.edu** or Google phrases such as 'accelerated learning'.

"Be positive about where learning is going to get them," advises psychologist Gaynor Sbuttoni. "If they can see it as a means of getting where they want, they're more likely to get on with it."

Gaynor also has some tips on how to help your child concentrate. "If they can't do this, there might be an intellectual reason or an emotional one. Ask them why they can't concentrate. If they say 'I don't know' the best thing to do is make an observation about their behaviour. So you could say something like 'Your teacher is concerned that you don't concentrate. What do you think? Do you agree?' This way, you're trying to open up their mind to thinking about what they're doing. You might not change them overnight but you're making them address the situation."

Some children, adds Gaynor, don't concentrate because they don't understand something or have a hidden learning problem. "Ask school for an internal assessment by the special needs teacher. This might not be as in-depth as an educational psychologist but it will give you some idea if there is a problem and, if so, where. If it needs taking further, ask school to recommend an educational psychologist or contact the British Psychological Society which has a list. If your teenager is reluctant to go along, tell them that they haven't tried this before and that if they really don't want to go again, they don't have to."

More advice on how to ~~kick them up the...~~ help them

The website **www.direct.gov.uk** has some useful advice on methods to help your child study and learn:

- Suggest doing homework as soon as it is received so that the information is fresh in your child's mind from classes.

- Encourage your child to speak up when in difficulty, as you may be able to help find the answers.

- Make sure your child has a good work-life balance and doesn't spend too much time going out with friends or sitting and doing homework (I wish).

- Find out about educational programmes on radio or television.

- Find out if there are any study support or homework clubs to help.

Coursework

Good coursework, points out DirectGov can boost your child's grades. You can help by:

- Finding out about the curriculum and how much work needs to be done.

- Finding out when coursework is due and helping your child to make a chart to complete it.

- Making sure your child is clear about what they are required to do and how marks are given.

- Finding internet sites and safe chat rooms that can help with studying.

- Encouraging your child to print and save work if they are working on a computer.

- Encouraging your child to talk to their teacher about any problems they are having as early as possible.

- Making sure your child has the right books and resources.

Take it from us

"When they tell you to get out of their room because they don't want you there, they mean it. And remember to duck." *Author*

"We found our boys concentrated better at school after we started giving them Omega 3 and Omega 6." *Julia, High Wycombe*

"I was shocked when I found that lots of parents in my daughter's year were helping their kids with coursework. I think it's a real cheat because there's an unfair advantage given to children of professional middle class families compared with children from families who show no interest in their work." *Jane, Buckingham*

"Be a listening ear. Be around for them to offload onto you.

This doesn't mean they expect you to solve their problems. They just want you to know how they feel." *Tom, Chester*

"Don't damage your relationship with your child by putting too much pressure on them." *Helen, London*

"If you worry too much about their school progress, they'll allow you to take that worry on and not learn self-responsibility." *Karen, Leeds*

"Our 18 year old son finds the studying hard. He therefore feels slow and stupid and imagines that people are impatient with him. He does, however, have some good friends which compensates. We use all sorts of accelerated learning techniques to help him study and feel good about himself." *Steve, Bedford*

THE EXPERTS SAY...

"Expect the best from your children but don't put too much pressure on them. Going to secondary school is the beginning of an awareness, for parents, that they are no longer in control. However, they still need you there. Rebellion doesn't go on for ever. It comes at different ages with different children so be on the look out!"

Bob Carstairs, Association of School and College Leaders (ASCL)

"Don't compare your children in front of them. Never say 'Your brother worked hard – why can't you?' Praise each one for their separate abilities. Don't even mention the other child." *Psychologist and mother Gaynor Sbuttoni*

Useful websites

www.englishspellingproblems.co.uk This is a site developed by Masha Bell, an English teacher. It has some great word lists for kids.

http://www.adprima.com/studyout.htm This is a great site for teaching study skills. It gives tips on test taking such as the 'memory dump' technique. This means writing down everything you've learned such as dates etc, on a spare piece of paper before writing essay answers. That way, you won't forget things halfway through. Other tips include answering the easiest exam questions first.

http://www.mind-mapping.co.uk/studying.htm. A good site for teaching your child how to mind-map; another way of remembering information.

THE EXPERTS SAY...

"Statistically, boys don't do as well as girls at secondary school. This is possibly because girls want to please and swot . But it changes when they get to university." *Bob Carstairs, ASCL*

CHAPTER 21

Getting your kids through exams

We all hate exams – unless we're closet geeks. And the problem is that many parents who remember their own fear and hatred of exams, pass the same feelings on to their kids. But now you're aware of where you've gone wrong, you can change. See exams as an opportunity for your child to show how much they know.

Here are some tips to get you going:

- Find out when your child's exams are coming up. Don't bother asking them because they'll probably pretend ignorance. Ask school or other parents.

- Try to encourage them to revise sooner rather than later. You stand a better chance of getting them to do this if they're still quite young and willing to listen. By the time they get to 16, they'll probably insist on doing it their way.

- If possible, read one of your child's English texts. Well, at least it's not a foreign language so you should be roughly on the same wavelength. You might then be able to slip in the odd question about George Eliot or helpful observation about Wuthering Heights while they're telling you to get out of their room and stop interfering in their life. When I had to spend an evening in casualty recently, I took with me my son's copy of *Silas Marner*. I finished it before I got to x-ray, which says a lot about our National Health Service. But it refreshed my memory since I hadn't read *Silas Marner* since my own school days. And now I'm able to fire questions at him over breakfast. It was almost worth straining a toe for...

- You could also spend a fortune on student guides which sell extremely well to parents who buy them in the belief that they can perform miracles in three and a half weeks.

- Try not to panic. You might be convinced that they're not going to pass because they've spent all their time on MSN or watching television. But kids nowadays are very good at multitasking. They can absorb information at the same time as all the social stuff.

- Instead, focus your energies on trying to get them to have an early night, eat nutritional food, know which exam they've got the next day, and have all the equipment they need for it such as a calculator or spare pen.

- Help them revise with exam techniques. For example, teaching them to visually remember a sequence of events in history or geography might help the information to go in. So too can drawing mind maps. There's an excellent range of books by Tony Buzan on this.

Stop them panicking

Psychologist and mother Gaynor Sbuttoni suggests encouraging your children to break down revision into manageable slices. "It's the feeling that they can't cope with it all that brings on panic. Help them work out a timetable and then break that down into smaller bits. If they don't want you to help, accept that for the time being. Teaching them to shut their eyes and breathe slowly is an old-fashioned remedy but it helps. Don't panic yourself – it will make them much worse."

We'd also suggest having a 'safety net plan'. I did this with my own children. Together, we'd work out a plan B if they didn't get the right grades, especially with exams which would decide their immediate future. For example, we'd have another school in reserve, or a gap year in case they didn't get the grades for uni. (The older two did. The third is about to do his GCSEs.) The safety net principle was important for both them and us. It meant that all was not lost if they didn't get the grades they hoped for. That in turn, took the pressure off so they performed better.

www.direct.gov.uk suggests easing the pressure of exams by:

- Helping your child to develop a timetable and then sticking to it.

- Listening to your child and finding ways to support them.

- Encouraging your child with praise and rewards.

- Creating a suitable environment for study and revision.

Take it from us

"Our son got reasonable marks during term but always got poor grades for exams because he found it hard to remember things when he was under pressure. We deliberately played it down and also encouraged him to write down key facts on a scrap piece of paper as soon as the exam started. It seemed to help." *Mary, Woking*

"When they're really tired with revision, give them an evening off." *Eve, London*

"My daughter always forgot which day she had which exam on. So I rang up school and asked for a timetable. She was very embarrassed and I was aware that I was probably interfering. But at least that way, I knew what she was meant to be revising for. The following year, she was much better organised so either I did something right or else she matured." *Hilary, Worthing*

"Make sure they have spare pens. My son ran out of ink and had to finish one exam in pencil. He got marks taken off as a result." *Sue, Manchester*

"If they're allowed snacks in exams, warn them not to spill drink on the exam paper. I gave my son a carton of orange juice and it ruined his maths sheet. He had to start all over again." *Christine, York*

"Don't start thinking you've got to do their revision for them. Some children want to be tested and others don't. Respect their decision. Exams is part of growing up and learning to take responsibility." *Sharon, Buckingham*

"Let them chill out during revision but discourage late nights." *Fran, London*

"Talking to me about exams helps alleviate my daughter's stress." *Name withheld*

"Playing the guitar helped my daughter chill out during exam revision." *Mary, Durham*

"To de-stress your child during exams, give lots of praise and encouragement." *Author*

THE EXPERTS SAY...

Psychologist Gaynor Sbuttoni advises: "If they really can't stand a particular subject – and are dreading it at exam time – sympathise with them. Tell them that you understand how much they hate maths or geography or whatever. But then point out that they can drop it after GCSEs. So the pain won't go on for ever. It helps them to know there's an end in sight. Also tell them that there are things that you have to do too which you don't like – such as filling in forms – but that once they're done, it feels better."

CHAPTER 22

Parents' evenings

Everyone should have a chance to get their own back – and this is yours. Seriously, even if you have a crucial office meeting or your youngest is in bed with the latest virus, it's pretty essential to get to a parents' evening. It's one of the few opportunities you'll have of getting one to one feedback. And, unless you have a pretty watertight excuse, you'll get a string of black marks if you don't turn up.

Many schools only hold parents' evenings once a year so you need to make the most of this opportunity. Organisation is the key word here. You might have been telling your child off all year about not being organised. But this is where you need to set an example. The first job is to get all your questions ready. Your child's school should have given your child a list of appointments with different teachers. They will probably have lost this list so try and find a duplicate or the original before you get there.

If you're meeting your partner there, after work, expect them to be late. Always save any you-said-you'd-be-there-on time's until later. Domestic spats don't look good in front of the teachers.

Ask your children if there are any particular points they'd like you to raise with their teachers. They will then tell you that the geography teacher not only fails to use deodorant but also hates them for no apparent reason other than the fact that they are always talking. This might be useful knowledge; forewarned is forearmed.

Take a notebook and pen so you can write down comments. Even if you're too stunned by what the teacher is saying to write something, it looks good. If your child is doing well at school, you can skip this chapter. If not, ask the teacher how he intends to improve your child's performance. When teachers tell parents how their children are doing, they tend to do so as though any fault lies purely with the child. In fact, this is a two way relationship and it doesn't do any harm to point this out in a polite way. You could say something like 'I understand that Susan isn't doing well at maths. What plans do you have in place to help her improve?'

Always try to be polite to teachers rather than having run-ins. Parents rarely win if they get cross or lose their temper. If you haven't already read it, go back and absorb Chapter Eighteen on how to get on with difficult teachers.

As children get older in secondary schools, they are often encouraged to go with their parents to these evenings. The plus side of this is that they can put their side of the story forward. Second thoughts, this might not be such a good thing if they're stroppy.

A note of warning: watch what you wear. A conventional outfit usually gives a better message than a short skirt or rainbow knitted hippie sweater.

Reports

If your child brings their own report home, you might have to nag them to show it to you. Ideally, get them to sit down and read it with you. It might send the message home.

Shouting and screaming won't help. Instead, calmly ask how they might improve and work out a plan for doing this. For example, you might get them to agree that they don't go on their computer until after homework in order to improve their grades.

It sometimes helps to re-read the report together before they start the next term. That way, they're reminded of the things they need to do – and not do. The trouble with reports at the end of term is that they are soon displaced by the sheer relief that it's holiday time and then all the advice (criticism?) is forgotten.

Finally, try not to compare reports with your friends, sister, neighbour or anyone else. You'll either end up feeling inadequate or you'll make the other person feel the same. Your child is unique. So is their report. Besides, some things are best kept to ourselves, don't you think? You can always hang it in the loo when they're famous.

Take it from us

"We pay our children for good reports and exam grades. I know it sounds like bribery but it works." *Viv, London*

"I keep all my children's reports in a file. I tell them that when they are famous and someone wants to print them, they'll thank me for it. My mother did the same with mine. I didn't become famous but my children love reading my old reports, especially the ones that said I could try harder. It also reminds me that getting a good report isn't that easy." *Amanda, London*

CHAPTER 23

Term dates and school holidays

The local education authority sets school term and holiday dates. If you're the kind of parent who loses the notes that your child gives you, you can look them up online at **www.direct.gov.uk**.

"Always write down dates as soon as you get them. You might think you'll do so later but you'll forget." *Martha, London*

Going away during term time

If you want to get an adult detention, you're going about it the right way. Holidays in term time can only be agreed by the head teacher or an equivalent. They can only agree to more than 10 school days' absence in any school year in 'exceptional circumstances'. It's definitely a good idea to discuss proposed holidays with school before booking that cruise to the Caribbean.

According to government guidelines, the following factors will be taken into consideration:

● The time of year for the proposed trip.

● If it's near exam dates.

● Your child's overall attendance pattern.

● Any holidays already taken in the school year.

- The age and stage of your child's education.

- Your wishes.

- The ability of your child to catch up on missed work.

- The reason why you're taking time off during term time.

A couple of years ago, during term time, my 15 year old son and I were in the departure lounge at Gatwick at 6am, about to board a plane to Malta. My son tapped me urgently on the shoulder and hissed 'Look!' To his horror, one of his teachers was in the queue in front of us. When he realised who was behind him, he looked as pleased as my son did.

"Where are you going?" he asked. When he heard our destination, he began to smile. "I'm going to Scotland," he said.

I'm not sure who was more relieved – the teacher or my son.

CHAPTER 24

School meals

Despite cutbacks, school meals are still available if you receive Income Support (IS) or Income Based Job Seekers' Allowance (IBJSA). If you are an asylum seeker, you will also qualify. To apply, you'll need to get a free school meals form from the local education authority (LEA). Your child's school might also have the forms.

Children who receive IS or IBJSA in their own right are also entitled to free school meals. All other pupils must be charged the same amount for the same quantity of the same item, although the meals may be subsidised. You should be able to get a form for free meals from the school.

Local authorities are not obliged to offer milk to pupils, but if they choose to, it must be free to those pupils who qualify for free meals.

If you're confused – and we wouldn't blame you – contact the local education authority. You can track yours down through **www.direct.gov.uk**.

There's been a lot of excitement in the media lately about children and parents rebelling against healthy eating in school kitchens. Here's our advice:

● Give them a healthy snack to take to school which is both good for them and which they like. They might need it if they don't like lunch.

- Don't panic. It's just one meal a day. Try and make sure they have a healthy breakfast and dinner.

- If your child needs a special diet, tell school before they start.

"So my daughter is a vegan with an allergy to lentils –
I take it that won't be a problem?"

Food facts

- Up to 10% of children are deterred from buying lunch at school by the cost (the average amount spent on a school meal is £1.46).

- Researchers in the US found students scored higher in tests when the nutritional content of school meals was improved.

- 70% of UK parents say there is too little time to prepare meals and then enjoy eating them as a family, so the school meal is the only opportunity many children have to enjoy eating as a social activity.

- Weight for weight, UK pupils eat four times as much confectionery as green vegetables.

- In an average class of 30 children, six pupils will not eat any fruit in a week.

- Around 1.8 million UK children are entitled to free school meals but more than 330,000 pupils don't get their entitlement.

We'd like to thank the charity Raising Kids for the above information. **www.raisingkids.co.uk**

In September 2006, the government set new nutritional standards for school lunches and other school food. These standards say that schools must:

- Make high quality meat, poultry or oily fish regularly available on their menus.

- Serve pupils at least two portions of fruit and vegetables with every meal.

- Limit deep fried food to no more than two portions per week.

- Remove fizzy drinks, crisps, chocolate and other confectioneries from school meals and vending machines.

CHAPTER 25

School uniform

If you are on income support, or fall into one of the following categories, you should be able to get a clothing grant towards school uniform:

● Income Support

● Income Based Job Seekers' Allowance

● Child Tax Credit, but are not entitled to a Working Tax Credit and your annual income (as assessed by the Inland Revenue) is less than £14,155

The clothing grant is £31.35 if your child is over 11 years old, and usually has to be spent at certain shops.

Canny school uniform tips

● Find out if the school has a second hand shop. You can get some great bargains.

● Don't be too proud to accept hand-me-downs from neighbours whose own kids go to the same school and have conveniently got bigger.

● Shop around. If you don't have to get an exact brand, go to one of the chain stores offering competitive prices.

● Quality is important. But remember that if your child isn't going to draw on their shirt or rip their pockets, another kid will do it for them. So is it really worth buying the best?

- Don't be different. Your kid will get a detention or be teased if they don't wear what the others do.

- Label everything. It will get lost. Trust us.

Take it from us

"I found it really hard to label my daughter's school shoes because you can't easily write in the sole. Then I thought of scoring her initials in the sole of the shoe. You have to be careful not to make a hole." *Julie, London*

"I can't sew so I buy those iron on labels instead." *Marion, Hastings*

"I use a black felt tip marker which won't run in the wash. I label everything with it." *Andrea, Luton*

"My son was always getting order marks for forgetting his tie. So I bought two from the second hand shop as spares." *Sue, Hemel Hempstead*

CHAPTER 26

It's an age thing

Any teacher will tell you that there are certain ages or years when children are particularly challenging. This could be to do with hormones or it might be because of pressures at different periods of their school career. But if you know when to expect these problem years, you'll be prepared.

Year 7

Year 7 is clearly a tricky time since children are still settling in. Your child is making new friends and coping with a completely different standard of work. They're also expected to get themselves to the right classroom, instead of being in one room where different teachers come to them. And they have to learn to hand things in on time. In fact, you wouldn't blame them for handing in their notice, would you?

On the other hand, it might be reasonable to expect your child to have settled down by Christmas. So if they haven't, it'd definitely be worth talking to the year head.

Kids also tend to muck around in class or play the fool in order to endear themselves to their peers. "One of our daughters learned that she could make people laugh in class and so she was constantly doing this and not working," said a mother who didn't want to be named. "A teacher finally pointed this out to us at parents' evening so we had a strong word with her. It seemed to sort it out."

THE EXPERTS SAY...

"Get a rucksack for all the heavy books pupils are given. Be careful your child doesn't develop shoulder problems from Year 7 onwards." *Victoria, teacher, London*

Year 9

"This is another renowned stage for problems," says Mandy Haehner, London teacher and spokesman for the National Association of Schoolmasters Union of Women Teachers. "It's when all their hormones are bouncing around. It really helps if parents keep communicating with them. Talk to them even when they grunt back. Find out what they find difficult and try to tackle this with the school's help. Read their homework diary and ask if they've done the homework they should have done. This is also the year when they have to decide on options for their GCSE courses. Discuss these with your children and get advice from school if necessary."

"By Year 9, pupils know whether or not they are going to be academically successful and this can cause behavioural problems as they come to act in the way they see themselves. We had this with one of our daughters. Try to focus on the things they are good at, to increase their self-esteem." Anna, London

Year 11

This is crunch time for GCSEs. It's also when parents start to bite their nails and wonder what will happen if their kids don't make the grade. "I didn't think my daughter was doing enough work," confessed Melanie from Woking. "I kept nagging her, hoping this might help. But it did the opposite and we had constant arguments. In the end, my nagging got her so uptight that she was really nervous when she took her exams. Her final grades were OK but I'm sure she could have done better if I'd laid off a bit."

There's also the severe likelihood that your son or daughter might have Fallen In Love. This is exactly what you don't want to happen around exam time, but Cupid and teenagers have other ideas. "I was really worried when my son started what seemed like an intense relationship with a girl just before his GCSEs," said April from London. "But in fact, she had exams too and wasn't allowed to see my son until she'd done a certain amount of revision every night. That made him revise too."

"My daughter wasn't organised enough with her coursework and left it all to the last minute. Sometimes you have to let them make their own mistakes. She had to retake two subjects." Tony, Cardiff

Year 12

In our day, the lower sixth was reasonably relaxing. But under the new A level scheme, where pupils take exams that count towards their final grades, there's no let-up. As a result, children can get very stressed. Our unenviable job as parents is to tread that fine line between supporting them and making sure they do enough work.

The best advice we can offer is to be there with marmite toast in one hand, and a stop watch in the other. Try to encourage them to work a reasonable number of hours without overdoing it or underdoing it. It might mean taking it on the chin when they're rude to you but that's often because they are pressurised. If you remember that and put yourself in their shoes, it might be easier.

Year 13

No surprises here. It is, after all, the final year where university applications have to be filled in and exams taken. Try the following tactics to reduce stress:

- Feed them.

- Encourage them to have early nights.

- Allow them to have chill time.

- Don't get too upset when they're rude.

- Be around in case they need you.

- Help them to be organised. Provide folders and wall charts.

- Get them to fill in forms ahead of deadlines. So the Ucas form has to be in by January. Persuade them to get it in much earlier.

You might also find our book *What Every Parent Should Know Before Their Child Goes to University* very useful (White Ladder Press, £9.99).

Take it from us

"In our experience, Year 13 was the most difficult because our son could have done with more help on study skills."
Name withheld

"Both our girls got stressed, especially during coursework in Year 11. What helped? Keeping to a sound routine with homework and always having interesting things going on outside school. Also knowing they had our support and that they could always talk to us, even if they were behaving badly."
Christine, Slough

"I think we should understand how much pressure children are under throughout their school career. All too often, we're on their back, asking them if they've done all their work. Sometimes they need time to chill." *Karen, Newcastle upon Tyne*

"Remember that every child is different. What works for one of your children at Year 11 might not work for another. Be prepared to be flexible but, whatever happens, keep working at a good relationship with them." *Mandy, Buckinghamshire*

"Don't be afraid to give them their freedom. Secondary school is a wonderful opportunity for them to make a wide circle of friends. Let them enjoy it as well as encouraging them to work hard." *Jan, Isle of Wight*

"Don't get on the wrong side of the teacher. One of my friends did this on his first day and the teacher has disliked him ever since. Now he's in the sixth form and needs this teacher's help for filling in his uni form. But they have a really bad relationship." *Adam, 16*

"Listen. Don't muck around." *Matt, 18*

CHAPTER 27

16 plus

Just when you've got over the hurdle and hassle of finding the right school for your child at 11, you might well find yourself having to do the same thing all over again at 16.

If you haven't reached this stage yet, don't skip the chapter. You might assume your child is going to stay put at their current school. But trust us. Things can change. The school you chose at 11 might not have the options they want by the time they get to sixth form level. You might be moving areas. Your offspring might have decided they want a change. Or – and this can happen – the school isn't that keen on having them any more.

Where to start

The good news is that you're not a newcomer any more. In fact, you're third handers. You've already waded through the maze of primary and secondary schools. And now you've got a better idea of what you're looking for.

The difference is that your 'child' is now almost an adult in their own right. So they'll have their own priorities too, such as the proximity of a new school to the nearest Pizza Parlour, and whether their best mates are going there too. Somehow you have to reach a compromise. And, as we all know, this isn't a word that features in many teenagers' vocabulary.

What do they want to do?

At the time of writing this, my very own 15 year old has three ambitions in life. To live in a van. To be a rock guitarist. To read graphics at uni. You can imagine which option I prefer. Yes of course it's the rock guitarist one…..

Seriously, before visiting schools or colleges, the most important factor is to check they offer the subjects your child is interested in. To do this, you need to ring them up and request their prospectuses. When they arrive, you'll find that AS and A levels are listed in blocks. Usually you have to choose a certain number of subjects from each block. Don't assume, either, that just because a school offers a subject, your child will be able to do it. There may well be limited places.

It's also important to have the right mix of subjects. If your child has any idea about what they might want to do afterwards, they need to check what qualifications they'll require. And this means making sure they're doing the right A levels. So you can see that you need to do a fair amount of research, not to mention pinning your child down to work out their own plans for the future.

AS and A levels

If you are still unsure about what an AS is when it's at home and are too embarrassed to put up your hands and ask, here's a basic rundown.

A few years ago, the government in its wisdom changed the A level syllabus. Instead of having three A levels which were sat at the end of the final year of the sixth form, most children now take four AS levels at the end of the first year in the sixth form. They then drop a subject and take three A levels at the end of the final year.

Actually, it's more complicated than that. Just like GCSEs, coursework plays a crucial part in these exams. Not only that, but the exams themselves are divided into modules so your child might be sitting one batch of exams in January and then another in May and June.

Each AS and A level carries a set number of points, depending on the grade. These are all totted up at the end of the two years and it's these that decide whether your child will go to the university of their choice. If they don't get the hoped for number of points after a module, they can resit. The advantage is that they can then hopefully increase their score. The disadvantage is that they might be taking rather a lot of exams in the long run.

"My daughter started off doing four AS levels because that's what most other pupils were doing. But she found it too difficult, especially as her subjects had a lot of coursework. So she dropped a subject. I was really worried in case it affected her chances of getting into a good university. But dropping that subject meant she could concentrate better on the other three and she got a good set of grades in the end. So don't assume it's the end of the world if your child drops an A level." John, Liverpool

Who can help you choose the right sixth form?

Start off with the school your child is already at. Find a member of staff you get on with or speak to the year head. Ask them to talk frankly about your child's strengths and weaknesses. They've had them for the past five years so they should know something.

Is there a careers advisor at your child's school? Talk to them too. Also talk to the local Connexions Centre, a government centre to help children make decisions about schooling. Tel 08080 013219.

Talk to other children and parents. Yes, their views will be subjective but you can still get some idea of a school or college's pros and cons.

Also look up Ofsted reports on schools and colleges you're considering. They list strengths and weaknesses in great detail. Also look at the Post-16 Tables (part of the Achievement and Attainment Tables) which should be available at the library, through your local education authority (LEA) or online. They will show results in general, and vocational AS and A levels, Key Skills at level 3, Advanced Extension Awards, other advanced vocational qualifications and intermediate vocational qualifications.

Your child will need to get a minimum number of points to get into a sixth form school so ask the school what these are. They should be spelt out in the prospectus. Some schools also ask for a report from the old school. You could always use this as a carrot or beating stick to get your child to pull up his socks.

You'll also need to decide if a sixth form college or school will suit your child best. A college might have a wider range of subjects and may well have a lower admissions criteria. The advantage of a college is that everyone is starting at the same time so no one feels like the new boy or girl.

Find out when each sixth form has an open evening and go along. It's worth checking out the dates as soon as possible in the academic year because some schools are so oversubscribed that they have only one open evening.

If you didn't manage to get your child into your first choice school at 11, you might find that you can get them into that school at 16. That's because every school has children who decide to leave at 16 and go elsewhere. So you can try to jump in, even if you're outside the catchment area.

The sixth form can also give your child a chance to mix with the opposite sex. This might or might not be a bad thing and sometimes only time will tell. My eldest son is still angry with me for sending him to a single sex school because he claims he didn't meet any 'fit' ones until he went to uni.

Questions to ask at prospective sixth form schools and colleges

- My son/daughter wants to do the following subjects for A level. Is this possible?

- What grades do they need to get, and in which subjects, to achieve this?

- If they want to do a subject that's not on your curriculum, do you have links with neighbouring schools?

- What is your policy on discipline?

- What are your drugs and smoking policies?

- What percentage of pupils do four AS levels as opposed to three? (This will indicate how academic the school is.)

- What do you do if a pupil doesn't do very well in AS levels? (Some schools actually ask pupils to leave because this will affect their league table performance. The problem with that is that your child will then have to find a school that can take them on, or else start the two years all over again.)

- How many new pupils will be starting the sixth form this year? (You don't want your child to be the only one.)

- Which schools do they usually come from?

- If a child is underperforming, what will the school do? How will they let you, the parent, know?

It might be worthwhile financially for your child to go into the sixth form. If your child is in the sixth form and your income is limited, they might be entitled to the Education Maintenance Allowance (EMA). It's also available for those starting an LSC funded Entry to Employment programme or a course leading to an apprenticeship. Contact your LEA or ring 0845 602 2260.

CHAPTER 28

So what do you want to do after school?

'It's my life!' This is a favourite phrase which my children constantly throw at me. And they're right. You may hope that they'll become lawyers or brain surgeons but they might well have other ideas. They don't need to make a final decision for life at this stage, but the choices they make at school will affect their options later.

"Don't impose your career aspirations on your kids," warns psychologist Gaynor Sbuttoni. "It's not fair and even if they follow your 'advice', they might end up resenting your interference later on in life. I've seen children who say 'I'm going to be an accountant because that's what my dad is and he wants me to be the same.' But in fact their strengths might lie in a totally different direction. So although you think you're helping, you might be doing the opposite. Just because you know about your own subject or work, doesn't mean they can't explore other areas that you aren't familiar with."

You can, however, help them see what the options are. Most schools give careers talks or set vocational tests which are meant to show a child's strengths. Follow these up and encourage them to do work experience in these areas to see if they like it.

"If your child doesn't want to go to university, it's not the end of the world," says psychologist Cary Cooper. "There are lots of other things they could do instead to fulfil themselves. Besides, many kids go on to further education later on, when they feel ready."

You can, however, give them tasters. Most schools organise work experience placements but, if you work, how about taking them to your office to see what you do? It might not be their cup of tea but they might just have more respect for what you do all day.

You could also leave careers notices and uni prospectuses lying around. Just a subtle hint of course… If you know older children who have gone on to uni or found a job they enjoy, try and get them to talk to your own offspring. They're more likely to listen to someone who was born within a decade or so of themselves.

CHAPTER 29

Your experiences at school – and how not to let them influence your child's school life

It's amazing how strong our own memories of school can be, even after several years. "I hated school because I didn't consider myself as clever as everyone else," wrote one parent from Kent who wants to remain anonymous. "Without realising it, I passed this dislike of school down to my own daughter. It wasn't until she asked to be moved to a sixth form college that she really enjoyed herself. I relaxed too and then she began to get better grades."

"Just because you liked or disliked something about school, doesn't mean your own children are going to do the same," points out psychologist Gaynor Sbuttoni. "Every child is different."

Schools can change – something we sometimes forget. If you went to a grammar school, don't expect today's grammar schools to be the same as your old school. The same goes for other kinds of schools too.

Take it from us

"I was unhappy at school because I was bullied. Luckily, our children weren't. But when we chose a school, we went for one which was prepared to nurture all kinds of talents, even if they weren't academic. It was the right decision because it made our kids feel good about themselves." *Ann, Isle of Wight*

"I disliked my school because it was very academic and I wanted a vocational career instead of going to uni. As a result, school lost interest in me. However, when I had my own children, we were still in the same area so my husband and I looked round the school. Fifteen years on, I liked it much better so we sent our children there – and they're very happy." *Ali, Rickmansworth*

CHAPTER 30

Enjoy it! School is meant to be the happiest time of your life

But is it? We know from too many children and parents that this isn't always the case. Neurolinguistic expert Heather Summers has the following tips to help your kids feel happier. Show them to your lot and see if it makes a difference. As well as being a mum, Heather is also co-author with Anne Watson of *The Book of Happiness* (John Wiley, £9.99).

Tips for children to be happy at school

Make the most of your surroundings

- Find time to be with people you like and whom you admire.

- Notice at least one thing that makes you feel good on the way to and from school each day. It could be a flower, a bird, a pet...

Choose what you do carefully

- When things don't go your way, choose how to respond. Ask yourself: What's good about it? How can I look at this in a better way? What can I learn from this? This strategy will make you feel more powerful and happier than allowing yourself to feel helpless and miserable about what happened.

- Find time to have fun during the school day – even if you are studying hard.

- Go out of your way to help others from time to time. This will make you feel good and you will find that people respond positively to you.

Develop your skills

- School is all abut learning new things. Be careful to choose subjects you enjoy. If you have a choice of topics for a project, choose the one that interests you most. The more you enjoy learning the easier it is, the more successful and happier you will be.

Stick up for what is important to you

- Don't be persuaded to say and do things you know are not right. This may be hard at times, but you will feel a lot happier in yourself and you'll sleep better at night.

Be yourself

- Trying to be what you think other people want you to be will make you unhappy – after all they probably all have different views. No one is perfect.

- Like yourself for who and what you are.

Be purposeful

- Set yourself some challenges or goals for the future – whether it's this year, next year or 10 years from now. This will make you feel that there is purpose in your life and that you have a value. You will feel happy and worthwhile.

CHAPTER 31

Our survey said...

At White Ladder, we're always keen to find out what *you* think. So we persuaded (bent arms) as many parents as possible to fill in a survey about their experiences of secondary education. The questions are below. We ~~begged~~ asked 19 year old Belinda Bates, a product of secondary school education and now at Oxford University, to analyse them for us.

Which of the following factors was most important to you when choosing a secondary school for your child?

a) Reputation   58%
b) Location   27%
c) Other   11%
d) League tables   4%
e) Ofsted   0%
f) Single/mixed sex 0%

In the final question some parents say it mattered whether a school was single or mixed sex, but no one ticked the option here

Which of the following, was the biggest problem when your child started secondary school?

a) Learning to be organised 48%
b) Making new friends   24%
c) Making the transition   19%
d) Working at a higher level   9%

e) Bullying   0%
f) Other   0%

Has your child ever been bullied by a teacher at secondary school?

Yes   24%
No   76%

Of those who answered yes, 40% said their child has asked them *not* to complain in case the teacher took it out on them.

How many schools did you look around, before choosing one for your child?

1 school	16%
2 schools	16%
3 schools	42%
4 schools	5%
5+ schools	21% (including one that was as high as 20-30)

Did you get your first choice?

Yes   80%
No   20%

Which of the following years, were most difficult for your child as they progressed through secondary school?

Year
7   26%
8   21%
9   26%
10   16%
11   11%
12   0%
13   0%

Are you happy with your child's secondary school?

Yes   100%

Is your child happy at school?

Yes   100%

Do children get too much coursework, in your view?

Yes   28%
No   72%

Does your child get stressed at school?

Yes   55%
No   45%

Are you happy with the present GCSE and A level system?

Yes   47%
No   53%

Were you happy at school yourself?

Yes   80%
No   20%

Did your own experience of school influence your choice of school?

Yes   70%
No   30%

Survey conducted by Belinda Bates
Entertainments Chair for Lincoln College

Useful contacts

You'll find all the websites referred to in this book on our website at **www.whiteladderpress.com** to make it easier for you to access them. Click on 'Useful contacts' next to the information about this book.

Contact us

You're welcome to contact White Ladder Press if you have any questions or comments for either us or the author. Please use whichever of the following routes suits you.

Phone 01803 813343 between 9am and 5.30pm

Email enquiries@whiteladderpress.com

Fax 01803 813928

Address White Ladder Press, Great Ambrook, Near Ipplepen, Devon TQ12 5UL

Website www.whiteladderpress.com

What can our website do for you?

If you want more information about any of our books, you'll find it at **www.whiteladderpress.com**. In particular you'll find extracts from each of our books, and reviews of those that are already published. We also run special offers on future titles if you order online before publication. And you can request a copy of our free catalogue.

Many of our books also have links pages, useful addresses and so on relevant to the subject of the book. You'll also find out a bit more about us and, if you're a writer yourself, you'll find our submission guidelines for authors. So please check us out and let us know if you have any comments, questions or suggestions.

HOW TEENAGERS THINK

an insider's guide to living with a teenager

jellyellie

So you've got a teenager? I'm so sorry. Still, they were really cute once, and they'll grow up to be a credit to you. It's just these few years in between you have to get through. It's not so much the lack of conversation, or even the fact that they never open the curtains. It's the fact that most of the time you haven't a clue where they're coming from. They could be an alien species.

Until now. At last, a real live teenager is prepared to communicate (yes, actually communicate) about what makes teenagers tick. Fifteen year old jellyellie dishes the dirt on what she and the many fellow teenagers she interviews really think. Essential reading for all parents, she explains what teenagers think about:

- school
- friends
- money
- designer clothes
- sex and drugs

...and all the other things that feature strongly in teenage life. She tells you what encourages teenagers to co-operate with their parents and what pushes all their rebellious buttons.

jellyellie hit the headlines two years ago when she launched her hugely successful website all about bluejacking (don't ask).
Described by the *Guardian* as 'the voice of the msn generation' she's back to tell parents how to get the best possible relationship with their teenager without simply giving them everything they ask for.

£7.99

Tidy Your Room

Getting your kids to do the things they hate

Are you sick of yelling at the kids to hang up their clothes? Tired of telling them to do their homework? Fed up nagging them to put their plate in the dishwasher? You're not the only one. Here, at last, is a practical guide to help you motivate them and get them on your side.

Parenting journalist Jane Bidder draws on the advice of many other parents as well as her own experience as a mother of three, to bring you this invaluable guide to getting your kids to do the things they hate.

The book includes:

- what chores are suitable at what age, and how to get them to co-operate
- getting homework done without stress
- where pocket money fits into the equation

Tidy Your Room is the book for any parent with a child from toddlerhood through to leaving home, and anyone who has ever had trouble getting their kids to do chores or homework. That's just about all of us, then.

Jane Bidder is a professional author and journalist who writes extensively for parents. She also writes fiction as Sophie King. She has three children, the eldest two of whom are now at university, so she has extensive personal as well as professional experience of getting kids to do the things they hate. She is the author of *What Every Parent Should Know Before Their Child Goes to University*.

Price £7.99

Index